Quanah Parker, Comanche Chief

THE OKLAHOMA WESTERN BIOGRAPHIES
RICHARD W. ETULAIN, GENERAL EDITOR

Quanah Parker, Comanche Chief

By William T. Hagan

UNIVERSITY OF OKLAHOMA PRESS : NORMAN AND LONDON

By William T. Hagan

The Sac and Fox Indians (Norman, 1958)
American Indians (Chicago, 1961, revised 1979; Hokkaido, 1983)
Indian Police and Judges (New Haven, 1966; Lincoln, Nebr., 1980)
United States–Comanche Relations (New Haven, 1976; Norman, 1990)
The Indian Rights Association (Tucson, 1985)
Quanah Parker, Comanche Chief (Norman, 1993)

Library of Congress Cataloging-in-Publication Data

Hagan, William Thomas.
    Quanah Parker, Comanche chief / by William T. Hagan.
      p. cm.—(The Oklahoma western biographies : V.6)
    Includes bibliographical references (p.   ) and index.
    ISBN 0-8061-2493-8
    1. Parker, Quanah, 1845?–1911. 2. Comanche Indians—Biography.
    3. Comanche Indians—History. I. Title. II. Series.
    E99.C85P3838   1993
    973'.04974—dc20   92-31563
                                                                         CIP

Quanah Parker, Comanche Chief is Volume 6 in *The Oklahoma Western Biographies.*

The paper in this book meets the guidelines for permanence and durability of the Committee on Production Guidelines for Book Longevity of the Council on Library Resources, Inc. ∞

1 2 3 4 5 6 7 8 9 10

*To Abby, Kate, Matt, Nate, Anne, Rachel, and Liz,
who have added a delightful new dimension to my life.*

Contents

Illustrations

Maps

Series Editor's Preface

WILLIAM T. Hagan's straightforward, readable biography of Comanche leader Quanah Parker is a revealing account of a pivotal figure in American Indian history. This volume not only clarifies the central role Parker played in the transitional decades surrounding 1900, it also supplies a balanced account of a classic "broker" figure caught between his Indian background and his increasingly important contacts with whites.

Drawing upon his thorough knowledge of Indian-white relations, reservation life, governmental policies toward Indians, and Gilded Age and Progressive Era conflicts in Indian Territory and Oklahoma, Hagan constructs a careful, revealing portrait of Parker. Describing his subject as a "middleman," the author demonstrates how Quanah retained his ties to Indian traditions in dress, religion, and family organization while accepting, even encouraging, negotiations with white cattlemen, processes of allotment, and new religion and educational practices of non-Indians. Discussions of factionalism and Indian-white squabbles that complicated and diversified Quanah's life are particularly illuminating. Step by step Hagan clearly delineates how Quanah learned to walk the white man's road and to benefit—and sometimes suffer—from this new direction in his life.

Overall, Hagan demonstrates that as a transitional figure moving from nomadic to reservation life Quanah Parker represents an approach not taken by other Indian leaders such as Chief Joseph, Sitting Bull, and Geronimo, who faced similar traumatic changes. In depicting Quanah as a cultural broker, Hagan avoids the excessively romantic Wild West accounts of earlier historians but also the plodding narratives of more recent writers treating postfrontier or bureaucratic topics. Hagan's solid, well-organized life story illustrates the dilemmas, conflicts, and troubled decisions that perplexed Quanah Parker throughout his life.

Hagan's biography admirably fulfills the dual purposes of the Oklahoma Western Biographies series: it traces the life of a notable westerner while it also demonstrates how that life shaped and now illuminates a significant period in the history of the American West. Likewise, this volume furnishes still another example of the thorough research, clarity of presentation, and balanced perspectives that mark Hagan's earlier essays and books. In William T. Hagan, Quanah Parker has found a sympathetic and probing biographer.

RICHARD W. ETULAIN

University of New Mexico

Preface

QUANAH Parker was the most publicized of the Southern Plains Indians of the reservation era. More than that, he had become by 1890 the most influential chief at the Kiowa, Comanche, and Wichita agency. His reservation career illustrates the terrible difficulties Indians and their leaders confronted at this stage. Quanah succeeded as chief because of his remarkable talent for seeking out the middle ground. A progressive on economic and political issues, he maintained his standing as a Comanche by refusing to reject important aspects of his tribe's culture.

Writing a biography of an Indian such as Quanah is a challenge. There is at once a wealth and a dearth of information on the individual. Of Quanah's life before he located on the reservation in 1875, very little is known. Once he came to the attention of army officers and Indian agents, it becomes much easier to track his progress. Within another ten years he was a celebrity, and more was known of him than of any other Indian on the reservation. But there is a downside. Virtually nothing is available to the researcher except that which has come through a white conduit. The observations on Quanah's activities and personality are usually those made by white men. Any Indian's comments have been recorded by a white man. Even Quanah's letters were written for him by white men or, late in his life, by an educated son or a white daughter-in-law. These individuals were endowed with varying degrees of education, so that at one moment Quanah sounds barely literate, and the next he comes across as a college graduate.

Given the nature of the sources, it is the public side of Quanah that we know best. The private side usually remains just that. When I first began my study of the Comanches in the 1960s, I was able to interview a daughter, Wanada Parker Page, and a son-in-law, Aubra C. Birdsong. Although it already was a half century after Quanah's

death, they were able to recall information about him that helped fill
in some of the blanks. Unfortunately there is much about his life that
we will never know, particularly the pre-1875 years and his relations
with his several wives. The public man's career is relatively easy to
follow, but Quanah's private life was rarely shared with the white
man.

Others have wrestled with the problem, and they are listed in the
sources. Without the foundation they laid, this task would have been
even more difficult. A variety of institutions and people have helped
me uncover materials or in some other way aided me in my efforts
to know Quanah and his people. They include staff members of
the National Archives, the Smithsonian's National Anthropological
Archives, the Southwest Region branch of the National Archives,
the Oklahoma Historical Society, the Fort Sill Museum, the Western
History Collections of the University of Oklahoma, and the Great
Plains Museum. Particular individuals to whom I am indebted include
Wahnne Clark, Kent Carter, Duane K. Hale, Jananita Pahdopony,
Towana Spivey, John Lovett, Robert Kvasnicka, and Mary Frances
Morrow. Jacki Rand has been most helpful in preparation of the
manuscript and index. My colleague Morris A. Foster, himself an
authority on the Comanches, read the manuscript and informed me
of his doubts about some of my interpretations. I also benefited
greatly from readings of the manuscript by Richard W. Etulain,
R. David Edmunds, and Thomas W. Kavanagh. Amy Forwoodson
incorporated the resulting changes in the final draft, cheerfully and
efficiently. As always, my wife, Charlotte (April) Hagan, has been
most supportive, this time venturing into the world of computers to
do the word processing chore.

WILLIAM T. HAGAN

Norman, Oklahoma

Quanah Parker, Comanche Chief

CHAPTER 1

Life on the Plains

ONE day in early May 1875 a young warrior named Quanah (Fragrance/Odor) rose in council to speak to his fellow Comanches. Distinctive in appearance, he was taller and less heavily built, and he had a complexion and hair lighter in hue than those of the typical stocky, dark-visaged Comanche. Confirming his mixed-blood origins were his startlingly gray eyes among a brown-eyed people.

The mood of the main encampment of the Quahada (Antelope) division of Comanches on the Staked Plains was one of quiet foreboding. What the white man would call the Red River War of 1874–75 was winding down, and most Comanches already had been forced to report to their assigned reservation and to surrender their arms and herds of ponies.

Word had filtered back to the Indians still free that many of the warriors and chiefs had been imprisoned, some of them in shackles in the narrow cells of the Fort Sill guardhouse, others loaded into wagons for the first stage of their journey to Fort Marion in Florida, a land beyond the ken of these Plains Indians.

Guided by three Comanches, a messenger from Colonel Ranald Mackenzie, who commanded the Fourth Cavalry Regiment headquartered at Fort Sill, had arrived at the Quahada camp the day before. J. J. Sturm, who for many years had been employed at the Indian agency to which the Comanches were nominally assigned, had been pleasantly surprised by the hospitality accorded him. In council the Indians did not protest Colonel Mackenzie's order for them to come to Fort Sill and surrender unconditionally. They did request a delay of one day before making a formal response in order to enable some of their leading men to return from a buffalo hunt and share in the decision.

Following that first council Sturm was pleased to be invited to the lodge of Eschiti (Coyote Droppings/Wolf's Rear End), the young

3

medicine man who had inspired the warriors attacking buffalo hunters at Adobe Walls in the Texas Panhandle in June 1874. Despite the failure of his medicine at Adobe Walls, Eschiti appeared to be the band's dominant leader, and he assured Sturm that he would prevail upon his people to follow Colonel Mackenzie's order.

The following day Sturm again met with the chiefs and headmen in council. He noted in his journal of his mission that Eschiti "told his people they must all prepare to come in to Fort Sill and as his authority seems absolute they all agreed to start tomorrow."

Sturm singled out in his journal only one other speaker at that meeting—Quanah, "a young man of much influence with his people," who also urged compliance with the colonel's order. Eschiti might have been the dominant figure in that village on the plains in May 1875, but in the reservation environment they were about to enter, it was Quanah who would earn the title, "The Chief of the Comanche Indians."

Very little is known with any certainty about Quanah's prereservation life, not even the origin of his name. There is no evidence that he ever visited his tribe's agency before the surrender in 1875, and only one white man seems to have seen him as a child. Late in life Quanah dictated a fragment of an autobiography, a few details of which were repeated in other interviews he gave. That he was not more forthcoming is not surprising. After his surrender Quanah was anxious to advance in the white-dominated reservation power structure, and boasting of his career as a young warrior with raiding parties that looted, raped, and killed their way through Texas and Mexican settlements would hardly have advanced his career. Such reticence was not unusual among former warriors. For years, Indian participants in the defeat of Custer on the Little Big Horn were, for fear of punishment, reluctant to talk freely to white men about their greatest triumph. Reservation officials in the early 1870s were continually frustrated in their efforts to assign responsibility for raids committed by bands under their jurisdiction. As admission of guilt could cost them annuities and rations, if not lead to their imprisonment, Comanche veterans of raids denied their own roles and attempted to cast suspicion on others—Kiowas and Kiowa-Apaches with whom they shared a reservation, or members of other Comanche divisions. The Quahadas were frequently saddled with crimes they had not committed because they rarely had direct contact with agency officials. This made them, as absentees, convenient scapegoats.

Quanah himself was a by-product of perhaps the most celebrated raid in Texas frontier history, an attack on Fort Parker in the Republic of Texas. The fort was occupied by the clan of John Parker, who had led his family from the Virginia piedmont on a hegira that lasted a

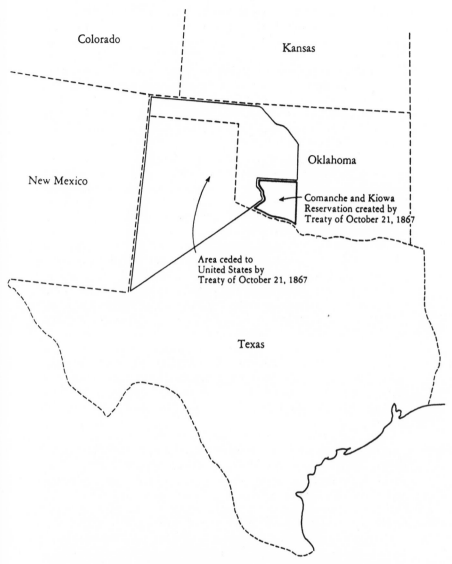

Colorado

Kansas

New Mexico

Oklahoma

Comanche and Kiowa
Reservation created by
Treaty of October 21, 1867

Area ceded to
United States by
Treaty of October 21, 1867

Texas

Reservation created by the Treaty of Medicine Lodge, 1867. (*From Hagan, United States–Comanche Relations: The Reservation Years, p. 40.*)

half-century and finally brought them to Texas, with residences along the way in Georgia, Tennessee, and Illinois. Elder John, as he was known for his leadership in the Primitive Baptist Church, had great-grandchildren by the time the family arrived in Texas. In late 1833 the Parkers established claim to land on the headwaters of the Navasota River. By the next spring they had cleared fields, planted their first crops, and constructed some crude log cabins. Work was then begun on a typical palisaded fort, which was completed in a burst of activity inspired by threats of Indian raids in 1835. With the successful conclusion of the Texas War for Independence, the settlers became overconfident and relaxed their security measures. On May 19, 1836, when a war party composed principally of Comanches and Kiowas suddenly appeared in the clearing before the fort, most of the men were working in fields some distance away. The gate of the fort was open, and the blockhouses unmanned. The warriors first feigned friendship and then quickly overran the defenses. Some of the whites escaped in the confusion, but the Indians killed and scalped three men and left three women wounded, one of them mortally. The dead included Quanah's maternal great-grandparents and grandfather.

The war party carried off five women and children, including nine-year-old Cynthia Ann Parker and her six-year-old brother John. Although there are other versions of John's fate, it is most likely that he died in captivity, as Cynthia Ann purportedly told one white man. It was common practice for these Indians to seize women and children. Some might be killed if the warriors were hotly pursued; often they were traded to other bands or tribes or exchanged for ransom. Cynthia Ann was one of those who remained with her captors, and with the passage of a few years became a Comanche herself.

Only four years after being abducted by the war party, Cynthia Ann was seen by a white man who was visiting a Comanche camp. Despite his having obtained Indian permission to talk to her, he was unable to communicate with the girl. For whatever reason—inability any longer to speak English, fear of punishment if she did, or a reluctance to do anything that might jeopardize her position in her new life—Cynthia Ann did not respond to the man's overtures.

In time, Cynthia Ann would become the wife of Peta Nocona, a prominent war chief, and bear him three children. She and they, but not Peta Nocona, were in a camp attacked by Texas Rangers in 1861. She fled on horseback with her youngest child, a daughter named Topsannah (Prairie Flower), but was run down and captured. Although assured by the rangers of kind treatment, Cynthia Ann was inconsolably grief-stricken at the separation from her sons and husband. Restored to white relatives, she was never reconciled to the loss of her Comanche family and the way of life of which she had become a part. Her daughter died within three years, and the unhappy Cynthia Ann in 1870.

Cynthia Ann had described Quanah as having a smallpox vaccination mark. Late in life he remembered a childhood incident in which a white man visiting his village was checking on the scar in an attempt to identify him. His lighter complexion and more slender build must have attracted the stranger's attention. Quanah dated this incident as occurring about 1862, before the death of his father. Horace P. Jones, whose long career as army guide, interpreter, and agency employee began on the reservation some Comanches occupied in Texas 1857–59, claimed twenty years after the event that he had talked to Quanah about his mother in 1868. They had met, according to Jones, when an army column he was accompanying had camped near a Comanche village. Neither account is verifiable. By the time Horace Jones's version was recorded, Quanah was well on the way to becoming a local celebrity, and many people were happy to try to associate themselves with him in some way.

We know little about Quanah's life before 1875, not even the year of his birth. In 1885 the Comanche agent estimated him to be not over twenty-five, but five years later the tribal census carried him as thirty-six. The confusion was compounded when the 1899 census listed him at forty-eight, but that age presumably became the agreed-upon calculation, as the government listed him at fifty-nine on his death in 1911. Accepting that computation as reasonable, we may conclude that Quanah was born about 1852 and was approximately nine years old when he lost his mother, eleven when his father died, and twenty-three when he was forced to give up the life of a nomadic warrior and hunter.

As the result of the work of scholars such as E. Adamson Hoebel and Thomas W. Kavanagh, we can be reasonably confident in sketching the type of life Comanches led when Quanah was growing up. In those years the Comanches were indeed lords of the South Plains. Quanah's division, the Quahadas, epitomized those fierce fighters and superb horsemen. They ranged from the Arkansas River in the north to the Rio Grande and beyond it deep into Mexico. On the west they approached the Rockies, and to the east they were feared as far as the edges of the heavily wooded areas of Texas and Indian Territory. Comanche wanderings were dictated by their need for pasture for their large herds of ponies and by dependence on the far-ranging buffalo herds, which provided the staple of their diet, coverings for their tepees, and raw material for tools and utensils. Additional incentives for their restless movements were provided by their insatiable appetite for horses and captives, which together with

Cynthia Ann Parker and daughter Prairie Flower, 1862. (*Courtesy National Anthropological Archives, Smithsonian Institution.*)

scalps and coups were the measure of a man in Comanche society. The horses and captives also were prized as important commodities in Comanche bartering with Pueblo Indians and itinerant merchants. By Quanah's time the Comanches had loose alliances with the Kiowas and that tribe's affiliated Kiowa-Apache band. To a lesser degree his people had a friendly relationship with the Cheyennes and Arapahos, who generally were to be found north of the Arkansas. In contrast, the Comanches intermittently fought the Utes and the Navajos and had a particular hatred for the Tonkawas, who served as guides for cavalry columns scouring the plains for bands the army dubbed hostile.

But it was the Texas and Mexican settlers who bore the brunt of Comanche fury. The Comanches particularly hated the Texans, who were slowly expanding into areas the Comanches had for generations regarded as their private hunting preserve, to be shared only with friendly tribes, such as the Kiowas and their allies the Kiowa-Apaches. During the Civil War years, agents of the United States were happy to see the Comanches ravaging the Texas frontier. But the fall of the Confederacy and the return of Texas to the United States fold did not deter Comanche raiders.

Nor was it possible, because of the loose-knit Comanche political structure, for the tribe or band leaders to restrain young men seeking war honors to establish their credentials in a society that judged a man by the size of his pony herd and the number of scalps collected and coups he had counted. Indeed, there was not the semblance of a tribal government. Unlike some other Plains tribes, the Comanches did not even have the tradition of gathering annually to celebrate the Sun Dance.

The basic Comanche political unit was the division, of which over a dozen have been identified. In turn, they were divided into residence bands, membership in which was determined principally by family relationships. These bands, however, were in constant flux as individuals and groups joined up or dropped away for an infinite variety of reasons. By the real beginning of their reservation period in 1875, the most important of the divisions were the Penatekas (Wasps), Kotsatekas (Buffalo Eaters), Noconis (Wanderers), Yamparikas (Root Eaters), and Quahadas (Antelopes).

By 1875 the Penatekas and the Quahadas represented the range of differences among the Comanches. Some Penatekas, whose band leaders had signed a treaty with the United States as early as 1846, had been persuaded to take up residence on a reservation in Texas in 1855. A nucleus of these had accompanied their agent when the hostility of Texas settlers forced the United States to shift their official residence north of the Red River to a section the government leased

from the Chickasaws and Choctaws, although it had been traditional
Comanche territory. A very few Penatekas even made spasmodic
efforts to farm, although most continued to use their reservation as
a base for their hunting—and raiding—expeditions.

At least the Penatekas provided some meager basis for the periodic
claims of Comanche agents to be gradually reclaiming their Indians
from what they considered a life of savagery. The Quahadas allowed
them no grounds for optimism, refusing even to come to agency
headquarters to share in the rations and annuities provided the tribal
members by the Treaty of Medicine Lodge of 1867. By that document,
signed by representatives of several bands, all Comanches were held
by the United States to have surrendered their claims to the South
Plains, except a reservation of about three million acres, and to have
agreed to locate on that tract together with the Kiowas and Kiowa-
Apaches. Although the Quahadas declined to come to the agency, a
stream of Indians from other Comanche bands, including Penatekas,
occasionally attached themselves to the Quahadas. Every spring as
the grass grew high enough to give the ponies strength to carry the
warrriors on raids into Texas and Mexico, or against the Utes and
Navajos, the Quahada population would swell, only to drop as the
approach of winter made the possibility of government rations more
inviting.

The Comanche political system gave considerable latitude to the
individual. Chieftainships were not hereditary, and any warrior could
aspire to head a band. The key qualifications were an outstanding
war record and a demonstrated concern for the welfare of one's
followers. But the chiefs had little real control, since band actions
were determined by a consensus of the headmen. Nor did all band
members necessarily accept the decisions the band leaders had
reached. If the matter was of sufficient moment, the dissenters might
secede, to join another band or establish the nucleus of a new one.

Although the Comanche way gave the individual great freedom,
it also imposed heavy responsibilities on its males. They were reared
to be the principal providers and protectors for a hunting and fighting
people. By the time he was five or six, Quanah was in training for
the role he would be expected to play. He would have been given a
small bow and encouraged to develop skill in its use. To succeed as
a warrior Quanah also would have to meet the standards of Comanche
horsemanship, and his fellow tribesmen were acknowledged to be
light cavalry with few peers on the plains. As a boy Quanah learned
to ride at breakneck speed while firing arrows or swinging low to
snatch objects from the ground. He and his youthful companions
heard the warriors boast of their exploits against the Utes, Navajos,
and Texans and yearned to emulate them. In this close-knit society,

respect by one's fellows was essential to a sense of well-being, and respect was earned the hard and dangerous way.

A Comanche's status also could be influenced by his claims to possess *puha* (power), which might be acquired in several ways. After reaching puberty, Quanah might have engaged in a vision quest. After preliminaries to prepare him, he would have retired to a secluded spot where he would have fasted, smoked, and prayed, all of which left him in a highly charged emotional state. What he sought was some sign that a supernatural being had taken note of his supplications and would share some of its power. A lone buffalo coming into view, a curious eagle swooping overhead, or a wolf howling in the distance might provide the youth with evidence that the spirit of one of these creatures had taken pity on him. He could than return to his people confident that he had acquired a powerful guardian.

An alternate way to power was to seek it, as Thomas Kavanagh has described the process, at a more mature stage. This could involve visiting the gravesite of one reputed to have possessed unusual *puha,* or even purchasing it or receiving it as a gift from the person so endowed.

In this quest for power, had he so engaged, Quahah would have been advised and counseled in this and other preparations for manhood by his paternal grandfather and other elderly male relatives. His father, Peta Nocona, provided a constant role model, although his own responsibilities as hunter and fighter took him away from the family for extended periods. In Comanche society, however, any uncles Quanah might have had would be addressed by the boy as father, and they in turn would refer to him as son. These father surrogates, together with the grandfathers, played important roles in the lives of Comanche youths.

That would have been the norm in Comanche society, but Quanah experienced unusual problems as he entered his teens. By then he had lost both his mother and his father. Another of Peta Nocona's wives had taken the orphan under her wing, only to die herself. Quanah remembered what followed as a painful and distressing period. He and his brother had no near relatives and were forced to scrounge for food and clothing. That this should have occurred in what is usually idealized as a close-knit society based on extended families was attributed by Quanah to his mother's having been a white woman. This is not an unreasonable explanation in a society in which, even today, "white man" and "Mexican" are slurs that can be directed at a Comanche of mixed-blood ancestry. As captive Texans and Mexicans were a common sight in Comanche camps in the mid-nineteenth century, such ancestry is not a rare thing.

Experiences such as he related could have driven Quanah to over-

come his social disadvantages by the one way open to any male—
excelling as a hunter and warrior, being more Comanche than the
full-bloods. That he had done so is evident from what J. J. Strum
observed when traveling to Fort Sill with the Quahadas. Quanah
spoke in open council, a privilege exercised only by men of some
standing in the band, and Sturm concluded that he was indeed "a
young man of much influence with his people."

After Quanah became a celebrity, he was described by white men
as having been a war chief or even head chief of the Comanches
before coming into the reservation in 1875. There is no basis for this,
and he undoubtedly was the beneficiary of the customary exaggeration of the youthful accomplishments of successful men. Quanah
himself was remarkably reticent about his exploits on the warpath at
a time when he must have participated in many raids against his
people's white and Indian enemies.

The fight with the buffalo hunters at Adobe Walls was one in
which Quanah acknowledged participating, even helping launch.
Many years later he related how the death of a friend at the hands of
Tonkawas scouting for a troop detachment from Fort Griffin, Texas,
caused him to seek revenge by organizing a war party. In the approved
fashion he took the pipe to camps of Comanches, Kiowas, and Cheyennes. Those who smoked with Quanah committed themselves to
accompanying him in his search for vengeance. But then chiefs inter-
vened to propose that the warriors first punish the buffalo-hide hunters who were making drastic inroads on herds upon which the very
way of life of the Plains Indians depended. That the Comanches, for
the only time as a tribe, were holding a sun dance that June is
indicative of their growing desperation as the line of settlement
advanced, troop columns penetrated the Staked Plains, and white
hunters littered the landscape with the skinned corpses of thousands
of buffalo.

As with other people in desperate times, the Comanches were
turning to a messiah, this one the young medicine man Eschiti. He
preached that the Comanches must fight or grow as weak and helpless
as the Caddos and Wichitas, who were trying to follow the white
man's road. He was so persuasive in his promise to provide supernatural protection from the white man's rifles that possibly as many as
three hundred Comanches, Kiowas, and Cheyennes, including several
prominent chiefs, agreed to join the expedition. Alone, Quanah
would have been able to mobilize perhaps a dozen warriors, and he
now found himself with a considerably diminished role in a major
war party.

The result is well known. At dawn on June 27, 1874, the warriors
attempted to surprise buffalo hunters gathered at the Adobe Walls

trading post in the Texas Panhandle. But a problem in the night with a roof beam in one of the buildings had most of the twenty-eight white men up and about when the Indians charged at dawn. Three whites were killed in the first rush; the others, however, quickly rallied and from the protection of the buildings kept the warriors at bay. Under cover and with ample ammunition, the professional hunters inflicted numerous casualties on the Indians, some of them at the maximum range of the heavy buffalo rifles. One of those wounded was Quanah.

Many years after the fight, Quanah told of having been in the initial dawn attack and having reached the buildings. He joined other warriors in trying to punch holes in the roofs so that they might fire on the occupants. Driven off, they were a few hundred yards away when Quanah's horse was hit, throwing him to the ground. Taking cover, he then was struck by a bullet, probably spent or deflected, that badly bruised his right shoulder, leaving it temporarily useless. A mounted comrade rescued Quanah, but his fighting was ended. By late afternoon the war party, which had lost at least a dozen killed, gave up its attack. Eschiti attributed the failure of his medicine to the fact that a member of the war party killed a skunk. Apparently this explanation was accepted by his fellow tribesmen because a year later he was the respected leader of the Quahadas that Sturm brought in to Fort Sill.

In the nearly a year intervening between the fiasco at Adobe Walls and the surrender at Fort Sill, Quanah must have participated in several of the engagements with troops and raids against Texas settlements that constituted the Red River War of 1874–75. The enthusiasm of some warriors ebbed rapidly after Adobe Walls, however, and there was a steady trickle back to the reservation.

It was becoming increasingly difficult for the Indians to maintain themselves on the plains. There was a severe drought that lasted from about mid-June until early September and kept the ponies poor. It also, however, delayed the army's movement against the Indians. A single unit was almost never capable of overtaking fleeing Indians on the plains, so the army had to resort to converging columns. Before the summer of 1874 was over, six detachments were crisscrossing the plains, trying at least to keep the Indians moving and deny them the opportunity to kill buffalo, dry the meat, and prepare hides for winter lodges.

As the troops tied to their supply trains plodded across the plains, the Indians usually had no great trouble keeping out of their way. On rare occasions, however, luck turned against them. Colonel Ranald Mackenzie, a commander who drove his men without mercy and was considered to be possibly the ablest cavalry commander of the post–

Civil War era, managed to penetrate one of the Comanche hideouts late in September. A large band had taken refuge in Palo Duro Canyon in the Texas Panhandle, but the troops, led by Tonkawa guides, managed to descend to the floor of the miles-long canyon before the Comanches were aware of their presence. Even then they escaped by scrambling up the walls of the canyon, although they had to leave behind their pony herd and all but a few of their possessions. Mackenzie, who two years earlier had inflicted one of the few defeats the Quahadas had suffered, only to have them later run off the ponies he had captured, made certain that would not happen again. He had over 1,000 shot, saving only about 350 to reward his Indian scouts.

As 1874 ended there were nearly a thousand Comanches enrolled at their agency, with some chiefs and warriors in army custody. Those regarded as most dangerous or guilty of raiding were incarcerated in the Fort Sill guardhouse. Others less culpable were lodged, under guard, in a partially completed icehouse, a roofless stone structure 150 feet by 40 feet into which were crammed about 130 prisoners. When Comanches came in to surrender, their ponies and weapons were taken from them, and some of the Indians were sent to the guardhouse or the icehouse. As the icehouse became overcrowded, inmates were released and assigned to the bands of chiefs the Indian agent and the army officers regarded as trustworthy.

Some of these cooperative chiefs and headmen were employed to try to contact bands that were still out. Before Quanah even reached the reservation, the Indian agent and army officers were singing the praises of Cheevers (Goat), Quirts Quip (Elk's Cud), and White Wolf, all Yamparikas, and Esahabbe (Milky Way), a Penateka. The last had won approval by bringing in 150 Kiowas in February 1875, the last large group of that tribe to surrender.

Colonel Mackenzie felt free to employ Indians, even those recently surrendered. He had put Coby (Wild Horse), a Quahada chief, in the icehouse in mid-April when he led a few followers in to the reservation. A month later, however, the colonel selected Coby and two other Comanches to guide J. J. Sturm to the main Quahada camp. Over the winter of 1874–75 the colonel also had concocted schemes to hire a Mexican trader to infiltrate the Quahadas and to employ a Kiowa hunting party under Kicking Bird as cover to get a cavalry detachment within striking distance of the Quahadas. Both Kicking Bird and the Mexican were to be rewarded from any ponies seized from the Quahadas. Neither of these stratagems was necessary because of the success of Sturm.

The white man's journal depicts the Indians as relieved once the decision to surrender had been made. Because of the poor condition of their ponies, they could only move slowly as they wound their way toward Fort Sill, hunting along the way. It would take them almost a month to reach the post, and Sturm sent Indian messengers ahead of the main party to let Colonel Mackenzie know that all had gone well. The messengers were led by one of the Comanches who had guided Sturm from Fort Sill and included that rising young warrior Quanah. The main body of the Quahadas did not reach Fort Sill until June 2, but Quanah arrived there with the other messengers the night of May 13.

That Quanah promptly sought out Colonel Mackenzie to seek information about his mother and sister is apparent from a letter the colonel wrote May 19. It was addressed to a quartermaster officer at Denison, Texas, seeking information about Cynthia Ann and Prairie Flower. The letter also was published in a Dallas newspaper and elicited at least two responses that Quanah's mother and sister were dead.

Colonel Mackenzie's expression of interest in the young Comanche mixed-blood is not surprising, given the favor he showed the Quahadas. The hard-bitten cavalryman had a grudging admiration for these stalwart fighters, who until now had refused to come into the reservation. Other bands, even Kotsatekas and Noconis, had been known to come to the agency for a few weeks at a time, drawing rations and annuities, and then, rested and resupplied, head off to raid in Texas or Mexico. After learning from J. J. Sturm that the Quahadas were coming in, Mackenzie wrote his superior, General Philip H. Sheridan, "I think better of this band than of any other on the reserve. . . . I shall let them down as easily as I can." And he did. The Quahadas were permitted to retain a substantial number of their ponies, and none of the group Sturm escorted ended up in the icehouse or the guardhouse. As a veteran himself, one who carried the scars of six Civil War wounds, the colonel admired fighting men of the quality of Quanah and his fellow Quahadas and could empathize with their plight.

The young warrior was a curiosity because of his white mother and his pronounced interest in her. That alone would have made Quanah a celebrity of a type. When coupled with his efforts to bridge the gap between the cultures while retaining his Comanche identity, together with his obvious intelligence and ambition, they would make him unique among the inhabitants of the reservations of the South Plains Indians.

CHAPTER 2

Quanah's New World

QUANAH'S world contracted distressingly when he took up residence on the reservation. For twenty-odd years the only home he had known had been the broad reaches of the South Plains, an area large enough to satisfy even the nomadic Comanches. It had contained some of the world's finest grasslands, which supported a wealth of animal life, including the millions of buffalo that the Comanches believed the spirits had placed on earth for their benefit. After they obtained horses, Quanah's people had had the mobility to exploit to the fullest this great space. In a week, villages could move a hundred miles to find the latest buffalo range or locate winter shelter and good water in one of the narrow valleys cut by the few streams. They lived well and enjoyed a freedom of which a white man tied to a farm or a factory work station could only dream.

Developed as a result of many generations' experience on the plains, the political and social fabric of Comanche life would gradually undergo change in the new environment. Some features of their life were more tenacious than others. The divisions, composed of residence bands, remained in place many years after the Indians came in to the reservation. Like the other Quahadas, Quanah and his wife and daughter who accompanied the Indians to Fort Sill in 1875 initially were carried on the agency's records as members of one of about twenty-five bands and subbands. Officials originally assigned them to Horse Back, a Noconi chief who had won the confidence of the military and the agent in charge of the reservation by his cooperation during the Red River War. At least as long as there were rations and annuities to be distributed, the band structure would be an important economic element in Comanche life on the reservation. Bands also would serve as the basic political unit, their chiefs being the links through which the Indian agent attempted to maintain control of the reservation's population. As in prereservation days, however, the bands were in a constant state of flux. A new element was the role of the agent in determining band leadership. It was within the agent's power to replace chiefs whom he regarded as obstreperous, or to encourage a chief's followers to move to another band, thus effectively reducing that chief's influence.

In theory the agent had virtually unlimited authority on his reservation, although the 1867 Treaty of Medicine Lodge had described his duties as merely those of a go-between to handle "matters of complaint by and against the Indians." The agent for a Sioux reservation once boasted that he controlled everything except the weather, although in reality agents were anything but omnipotent. Their tenure averaged only two to three years, so that, given their customary initial ignorance of the Indians to whom they were assigned, they usually did not last long enough to learn their job really well. And there were always elements on the reservation who had influence of their own. They included agency employees who had been around long enough to develop personal ties with the Indians, perhaps taking an Indian wife who would give them family connections and additional clout. These intermarried whites, "squaw men" in the jargon of the day, were in a position to facilitate or seriously complicate an agent's task. Others who developed power bases of their own were the interpreters, upon whom the agent usually was totally dependent, the traders, who might have dealt with the Indians during the tenure of several agents, and the unusual missionary who developed a loyal following. Finally, the officers commanding Fort Sill during the first few years sometimes had to be turned to for protection or to provide rations for starving Indians.

The agent also was beholden to those above him in what was a burgeoning bureaucracy. When Quanah became a reservation Indian, the head of the Kiowa and Comanche Agency, as it was labeled, reported to the central superintendent, who resided at Lawrence, Kansas. Even communications addressed to the commissioner of Indian affairs were routed through the superintendent's office. The commissioner, in turn, reported to the secretary of the interior, in whose office there developed an Indian Division, the head clerk of which actually made most of the decisions on matters referred to the secretary. The commissioner of Indian affairs might seem to the Indian agent to wield the power, but to those who knew the inner workings of the Indian service, the commissioner frequently appeared to be a highly paid clerk who transmitted requests and recommendations to the office of the secretary of the interior, and that office's responses back to the agents.

It could be argued that the real power to determine what happened at the Kiowa and Comanche Reservation was located in Congress.

That body determined the funding for the reservation's activities at
a time when the Comanches became dependent on government rations for their very existence. Until 1871 the Senate, and after that
both houses, ratified—and sometimes unilaterally amended—any
treaties or agreements between the tribes and the United States. The
Indian committees of both houses controlled the fate of proposed
Indian legislation. Patronage policies might vary with administra-
tions, but members of these congressional committees, not surpris-
ingly, had a major voice in the selection and retention of Indian
agents and other reservation employees.

Although power over the Indians and their reservations seemed
badly fragmented, there was consensus among government officials
and the private citizens who interested themselves in Indian affairs
on what should be done with the tribesmen. The Treaty of Medicine
Lodge of 1867 contained clauses found in other treaties of that period,
clauses that provided for the white man's brand of education and
ultimately the division of the reservation land among its inhabitants
in the form of private property. The underlying assumption of the
architects of those treaties was that within thirty years, with the help
of education, the powerful motivation of private property, which
would encourage greed (which was held to be inconspicuous in
Indian societies), and the inculcation of Christian values by missionaries, the Indians would be sufficiently acculturated to enter the main-
stream of American society.

For Quanah and his fellow Comanches their reservation in the late
1870s was a long way from being a nursery of civilization. Simply
surviving was the principal task. The theory had been that the Indians
would immediately launch into farming, although it was assumed
that it would be several years before they would become fully self-
supporting. In the interim they would continue to hunt, and supple-
mentary rations would be supplied by the government, although
there was no provision in the 1867 treaty for this. But the region in
which the reservation lay posed a real challenge even to veteran white
farmers. Droughts were common, and their effect was multiplied by
the hot, dry winds of summer. Corn, for example, a mainstay of
farmers to the east, is not grown even today in any quantity in western
Oklahoma. In the 1870s agents had corn planted and replanted, trying
to get a crop, but in most seasons only in bottom lands along streams
did they have much success. Even then lurking insects of intimidating
size and voraciousness seemed to consume whatever crops did mature. And fundamental to the problem was the aversion of Comanche
males to farming. They were reared to be hunters and fighters, not
farm laborers. Although more inclined to adapt to the changed condi-

tions than many of his peers, no one ever reported seeing Quanah with a hoe in his hand or trying to plow a straight furrow.

Hunting to supplement what could be raised had its own difficulties. In the first few years government officials were understandably chary of permitting Indians to leave the reservation to hunt, for fear that they would clash with the Texans. This became more and more a possibility in the 1870s as the Texas ranching frontier reached the stretch of the Red River that constituted the southern boundary of the reservation. Despite the likelihood of trouble, officials were unable to ensure sufficient rations, and the situation became so critical on several occasions that the Indian agent borrowed rifles and ammunition from the Fort Sill garrison and obtained cavalry escorts for hunting parties. The white hide hunters, however, were making such rapid inroads on the buffalo herds that these efforts were seldom very productive and ceased entirely after 1878. In the winter of 1877–78 the Fort Sill post commander had to send wagonloads of rations out to the starving Indian hunters, including a party headed by Quanah. In the future, even if little parties slipped away from the reservation, they could not find game enough to sustain their old way of life for more than a few weeks.

Under the circumstances government rations became absolutely essential. Unfortunately they were never available in sufficient quantity. The ration problem had become obvious at the Kiowa and Comanche Reservation well before Quanah took up residence there. Although it was soon apparent that the Indians could not or would not raise enough crops to make a difference, and that hunting was no longer a viable option, Congress failed to substantially increase appropriations for Indian support. Nor was the freighting system efficient enough to deliver on time what was purchased. In 1875 Fort Sill was 165 miles from the nearest railroad at Caddo, Indian Territory. Heavily laden wagons had trouble negotiating the trail, particularly after thaws or heavy rains. In those conditions, if they moved at all, wagons pulled by six or eight yoke of oxen would take more than a month to reach the reservation. Thus in bad weather the supplies tended to back up at Caddo, and no appeals from a desperate Indian agent could move them.

An action by a Texas congressman in 1875 had complicated the situation. He managed to attach to the Indian appropriation bill a rider that forbade the Indians to enter Texas. Enforcement of this legislation prevented hunting parties, even when escorted by troops, from crossing the Red River to locate the last remaining buffalo herds of significant size. This meant not only a sharp reduction in meat consumption but increased dependence upon canvas for tepee covers, a poor substitute for buffalo hides. Nor would the Indians any longer be able to trade buffalo robes for the goods of their reservation traders and the Comancheros. These latter—New Mexicans and Pueblo Indians—had for generations ventured out on the plains to visit Comanche camps to trade hard bread, blankets, and other commodities for buffalo meat and hides, and the captives, horses, and cattle seized in raids on the Texas and Mexican settlements. The last recorded visit of Comancheros was in the summer of 1880, when they sought out Comanche and Kiowa camps in a remote part of the reservation. The Swiss-American scholar Adolph F. A. Bandelier, who was just beginning his study of the Pueblos, recorded the departure and return of the Comancheros, whom he depicted as now finally accepting that the Comanches no longer had the commodities that had made the trade profitable. It was a historic watershed, the Comancheros passing from the scene as the ethnologists arrived. Officials were not unhappy to see the trade end, else, as one put it, their charges might be tempted to reenter "the horse business."

As the Indians came to depend almost exclusively on government rations, their agent spent more time trying to convince Washington authorities of the seriousness of the situation. Complying with a regulation designed to keep the Indians on a short leash, he issued rations on a weekly basis. The most important element in the ration was the beef component, supposedly one and one-half pounds per person per day, increased to two pounds in 1878. But this was beef issued on the hoof, with the animal estimated to provide in edible beef about 50 percent of its gross weight. Unfortunately, in the winter the range-fed cattle lost weight and strength to the point that some had to be helped from the corral, and their carcasses would provide much less meat than the 50 percent anticipated. Indeed, some were in such bad shape that the Indians got little more than the hide, which could be sold to the trader. A representative of the Board of Indian Commissioners, an oversight body created in President Grant's administration, reported inspecting one carcass from which, "by scraping along each side of the backbone, a pound of meat could not be got."

When the cattle were in their worst condition, the agent might try to compensate by adding some "mess beef," a poor quality salted so heavily that only a very hungry Indian could down it. Other ration components, principally flour, bacon (for which the Indians cared little), coffee, and sugar, also were often in short supply or nonexistent. Even if available, the rations were seldom sufficient to feed the Indians adequately for a full week. For the two or three days preceding issue day, Indians all over the reservation would be going hungry. The agent might borrow flour, sugar, and coffee from one of the traders, promising to repay the loan when the wagon train finally arrived from Caddo. Sometimes the agent would go hat in hand to Fort Sill to try to persuade the commanding officer to put himself at risk by providing emergency rations from army stores. Colonel Mackenzie made several appeals to his superiors for permission to issue rations to the Indians, on one occasion putting it in terms difficult to ignore: "The position of a jailor for a vast band of half starving criminals can never be pleasant, no matter how bad you may consider the criminals."

As long as rations were issued once a week, much Comanche time was consumed in drawing them. They lived up to twenty miles from the agency and customarily spent Thursday traveling there, Friday drawing rations, and Saturday returning to their camps. Such a schedule was not conducive to proper care of livestock or crops. The beef issue, however, did provide a little diversion to enliven their drab existence. The animals were released from a corral and then run down by the men and boys, who finished them off with bows and arrows or pistols, a pathetic substitute for the excitement of the buffalo hunt.

By 1878 the roughly three thousand Indians on the Kiowa and Comanche Reservation were supposed to be receiving weekly, in addition to their beef ration, 10,000 pounds of flour, 2,000 pounds of bacon, 825 pounds of coffee, and 1,650 pounds of sugar. More was needed, but Congress was disturbed at the growing expense and reluctant to appropriate funds to feed able-bodied Indians. In 1875 it had prescribed that Indians would have to work to receive rations, although the Comanche agent had been able to get an exemption for his Indians, pleading special circumstances. On other reservations as well the government found it preferable to feed rather than fight.

The agent and the superintendent in Kansas could not be faulted for being too harsh with the Indians or for failing to try to secure them more and better rations. Both were Quakers appointed under President Grant's policy of having religious groups nominate personnel for the Indian service. Agent James M. Haworth and Superintendent Enoch Hoag were dedicated advocates of the peace policy that stressed avoidance of force and appeals to the better nature of the Indians. Haworth was agent from 1873 until health problems forced him to resign in 1878, the same year Quakers lost control of the central superintendency. Those who found it a paradox to have a Quaker trying to control Plains warriors, tended to find him weak, indecisive, and too lenient, a failure as an agent. Those more sympathetic stressed his nobility of spirit, although they had difficulty pointing to much evidence of progress as it was measured for reservation Indians.

Agent Haworth was responsible for Quanah's first step up the ladder to the leadership of the Comanches. Primarily to simplify the issuing of rations, Haworth created additional "beef bands" to a total of thirty. To head one of them he chose Quanah in late 1875. The newly designated band chief proved cooperative. On one occasion Quanah was dispatched by Agent Haworth and Colonel Mackenzie to search for runaways from the reservation. After nearly two months he returned with a party of twenty-one that he had located on the Pecos River. The warriors were put in the Fort Sill guardhouse, and their ponies and weapons were confiscated. Quanah also secured Herman Lehman from the Kiowa-Apaches, a white boy in his late teens who had been a captive since 1870. Herman lived with Quanah as a member of his family for three years and looked upon the chief as his foster father. Then General Mackenzie located his widowed mother, and Herman was sent to be with her. He returned to visit Quanah on three occasions and in 1901 sought adoption by the Comanches, which he achieved finally with Quanah's help.

The new Comanche chief also made contributions in the struggle to cope with the plague of horse thieves. Some of them were Texans, or ranchers in the Chickasaw Nation, who had despaired of reclaiming their stolen stock through official channels. Most, however, were simply taking advantage of the presence in 1878 of over four thousand ponies easily accessible on unfenced pastures. Quanah led one small Comanche party that ran down thieves who had driven off nearly fifty ponies. Although the rustlers escaped, they were forced to leave behind four of their own mounts.

A year after that episode Quanah's band was accused of stealing Texas stock while out hunting. The chief's defense was to observe that their ponies were in bad shape when they had returned from the unsuccessful hunt; if they had stolen replacements, they would have taken better ones. That rang true to anyone familiar with Comanche knowledge of horseflesh and their ability to slip the best available from right under the nose of its jealous owner.

Despite such minor setbacks, Quanah's stature among the band chiefs rose steadily. By the end of 1878 he headed the third largest band, with ninety-three members. Quanah also now had three wives, an indication of at least sufficient means to acquire and support them. Wives were normally obtained by purchase, using ponies principally, as that was the most common form of property. The girl's wishes in the matter were usually a minor consideration. It also should be noted that as buffalo were becoming a thing of the past, plural wives were a luxury, as extra hands were no longer needed for the lengthy task of preparing hides and robes for the trade.

Quanah's domestic arrangements in this early period are not entirely clear. His first wife was To-ha-yea, a Mescalero Apache, al-

Quanah, ca. 1877. (*Courtesy Western History Collections, University of Oklahoma Library.*)

though she seems to have disappeared from the scene before 1875. The wife and daughter who came into the reservation with him that year must have been Weck-e-ah (Hunting for Something) and Nahmukuh, who later married a white man, Emmet Cox. A highly romanticized version of Quanah's courtship of Weck-e-ah has her eloping with him to avoid becoming the wife of an older warrior able to offer her father more ponies than Quanah could then afford. (This version, featuring a very buxom Weck-e-ah, has been enshrined in comic-book form.) The other two wives were Cho-ny (Going with the Wind) and A-er-wuth-takum (She Fell with a Wound), both of whom had four children by Quanah.

Supporting such a rapidly growing family was a definite challenge, given the straitened circumstances in which the Comanches found themselves. Being a band chief helped, as they were unlikely to be slighted in the distribution of rations and annuities. The latter were dispensed in accordance with the 1867 treaty, which provided for the Comanches sharing with the Kiowas and Kiowa-Apaches for thirty years an annual purchase of $30,000 in useful goods, plus a special allotment of clothing. The goods included such items as axes, frying pans, hoes, thimbles, tin plates, and butcher knives. Many of these items, as well as some of the clothing, the Indians would promptly sell to white men for a fraction of their value.

Quanah also could have been expected to have gotten at least his fair share of cattle and sheep purchased with money from the $27,000 Pony Fund. This had been created by the proceeds from the army's sale of ponies seized when the Comanche, Kiowa, and Kiowa-Apache bands reported in to Fort Sill. Colonel Mackenzie first purchased 3,500 head of sheep on the theory that they would be less attractive to the white thieves who preyed on the Indians. But the Comanches did not take to herding the wooly beasts or to eating mutton, and the sheep were forced to fend for themselves against dogs, coyotes, and the weather. Few survived the first winter. As the Indians were now eating beef, the four hundred cattle purchased were much better received. The idea had been to use them as foundation stock for Indian herds. Given unsuccessful efforts to stretch the rations for seven days, many of the cattle were sacrificed to meet immediate needs, deferred gratification not being a Comanche strong point.

Despite the problems of reservation life, within three years of his surrender to Colonel Mackenzie, Quanah was making his mark. Bringing in the twenty-one runaways had been lauded by Mackenzie as "excellent conduct in a dangerous expedition." At the same time, however, Quanah had insisted that those he brought in be confined on the reservation as opposed to being shipped off to Fort Leavenworth or elsewhere. This earned him the gratitude of the runaways, as he had relayed to them Colonel Mackenzie's intention to send some of them away to be imprisoned. In that fashion Quanah managed to win approval from both the colonel and those he brought in.

Further evidence of the colonel's personal interest in Quanah is a letter he wrote Isaac Parker, Cynthia's uncle, telling him of Quanah's wish to make contact with his Texas relatives. Mackenzie spoke sympathetically of Quanah's feeling that the Parkers were refusing to acknowledge him as a member of the family and said that Quanah "certainly should not be held responsible for the sins of a former generation of Comanches, and is a man whom it is worth trying to do something with." The colonel also reported that, "after an Indian custom," Quanah would like to receive a small gift from his Texas relatives as a signal that they would welcome a visit from him. There is no record of a response by Isaac Parker.

Not all Fort Sill commandants were so supportive of Quanah. Lieutenant Colonel J. W. Davidson did regard him as "undoubtedly the most influential man among the Quahadoz [sic], and one of the most influential among all the bands of the Comanches." Unlike Mackenzie, however, this colonel saw a darker side to Quanah. He was disturbed when the Quahada allied himself at a council with Big Bow, a notorious Kiowa raider. Colonel Davidson had called the council to get Comanches and Kiowas to accompany a cavalry detachment so that they might have pointed out to them the boundaries of the reservation. Quanah and Big Bow responded by calling into question the legality of the 1867 Treaty of Medicine Lodge, upon which the government based its relations with these tribes. Davidson warned his superiors that three years after the end of the Red River War the Comanches and Kiowas had weapons and ponies and "wear their arms in about the same way they did prior to the campaigns against them in 1874–75, although one object was to dismount and disarm them." The colonel concluded that "after our experience of late years with the Modocs, the Sioux and the Nez Perces, the latter our friends for over forty years, we cannot watch these Indians too closely, nor treat them too kindly."

Colonel Davidson had great hopes for the agent who replaced James Haworth in the summer of 1878. Philemon B. Hunt had risen to the rank of lieutenant colonel in the Civil War Union army, and Davidson expected to forge a better relationship with him than he had had with the Quaker Haworth. There was a brief honeymoon period, but then the normal bickering between individuals assigned to rival federal agencies took over. This was a period when army officers publicly criticized the inefficiency and corruption of the Indian service. Members of that organization objected to the officers' assumption of moral superiority and resented their own dependence on the army for the safety of themselves and their families.

Agent Hunt did share with Mackenzie and Davidson an appreciation of the growing importance of Quanah among the Comanches. Hunt was even prepared to try to help Quanah claim his rightful share of any estate his mother might have left. A report had reached the agent that the Texas legislature had voted Cynthia Ann a warrant entitling her to select a large grant from state-owned land. Attempting to confirm this while not alarming other heirs, he wrote Benjamin Parker, another uncle of Cynthia Ann's, on the pretext that he was curious to know more about the life of Parker's niece. Hunt also sought from his original informant a copy of the legislation, should any litigation be necessary. The affair dragged on for three years while he involved attorneys and a land agent in Texas. Quanah became interested in the project and pestered the agent for information as the months and years passed. The outcome was a disappointment, the Texas land office ruling that the warrant was void, having been issued while the state was in rebellion and the period for challenging such decisions having lapsed. Considering that the Austin land agent proposed selling the warrant for $500, retaining $250 for his services, it would appear that Hunt had unnecessarily raised Quanah's expectations.

Five years after the bands had united on the reservation, the son of Cynthia Ann had emerged as the Comanche leader most frequently consulted by the Indian agent. When the government proposed a merger of the Kiowa and Comanche Agency with the Wichita Agency, which included an additional eight tribes, Quanah spoke for the Comanche opponents of the reorganization. The government hoped to save money by the merger, but for the Indians it could mean as much as a fifty-mile trek to the new consolidated headquarters at Anadarko on the Washita River. Agent Hunt blamed Colonel Davidson for inspiring some of the Comanche opposition, although he also was concerned with Quanah's attitude. The young Comanche was by now the acknowledged leader of the Quahadas, the division Agent Hunt believed to be, "of all the tribes and tribal subdivisions in this section . . . perhaps the most warlike and dangerous if not treated judiciously." Not that Quanah was the answer to controlling the Quahadas. No chief among the Comanches had ever had that much authority. Quanah made this clear in a familiar plaint of tribal leaders when he told Colonel Davidson that he could not restrain the Quahada young men, this time relative to their desire to search for buffalo in the fall of 1878.

Nevertheless, there were occasions when Quanah would be helpful.

Once he apprehended a young Quahada who had attempted to kill a sentry at Fort Sill. And early in 1880 the agent was prepared to permit him to accompany a Ute captive of the Kiowas to Washington, if Quanah could get the Ute from Big Bow's camp. That excursion fell through when Quanah insisted on taking two of his wives with him.

In five years on the reservation, Quanah had come a long way. In May 1875 he had been, despite his youth, a leading man among the Quahadas, although still operating in the shadow of the medicine man Eschiti and other band leaders. By the spring of 1880, however, both the military and civilian leadership recognized that he had become the Quahada they must consult on important matters relating to that division, as well as being one of the most influential of all Comanche chiefs.

In some respects, nevertheless, he had not yet broken free from the pack. Other chiefs also had represented the Comanches and performed valuable services for the military and agency officials. White Wolf, Howeah (Gap in the Woods), and Tabananaka (Hears the Sun) also had spoken out in council against moving their agency north to the Washita. Eschiti, now usually referred to as White Eagle, to the confusion of historians, also had been credited with persuading runaways to return to the reservation. And Black Horse actually had captured the thieves who eluded Quanah, although losing horses to him. But already developing was a situation involving white ranchers and reservation grass that would offer enterprising and cooperative Indians abundant opportunities, and Quanah would make the most of it.

CHAPTER 3

Quanah and the Cattlemen

BETWEEN 1880 and 1883 the competition among white ranchers for reservation grass became the dominant issue in tribal politics on the reservation. It ultimately divided the Indians into proleasing and antileasing factions and contributed to the corruption of both agency personnel and Indian leaders. Quanah was actively involved as the principal leader of the proleasing faction, and he profited in that role, both politically and financially.

The Red River War was hardly over when Texans began driving cattle across the reservation. They followed the Western Trail, so called to distinguish it from the Chisholm Trail, which ran just east of the reservation boundary. The Western Trail crossed the Red River near the mouth of its North Fork and terminated at Dodge City, Kansas. As time passed, it bore a larger and larger proportion of the Texas cattle headed for Kansas. In June 1876 alone, Fort Sill's post adjutant reported that five herds were traversing the west end of the reservation. The problem would be complicated as the herd owners became aware that there was little to fear from dawdling for weeks on Indian land, allowing their cattle to recoup from a difficult drive to the Red River, or simply holding the herd in place on free grass while prices improved at Dodge City. The rapidly disappearing buffalo were leaving behind them excellent pasturage to be exploited by the enterprising, and these Texans were nothing if not enterprising. An agent's report on the reservation in 1878 described its "fine nutritious grass in almost inexhaustable quantities . . . plenty of water and good shelter." These were alluring possibilities to ranchers who, with each passing year, were facing more competition for good range south of the Red River.

In the late 1870s the Comanches, Kiowas, and Kiowa-Apaches had been discouraged from even hunting in the western part of the reservation, and their dependence on weekly issues of rations helped tie them to the agency. This resulted in only the eastern portion of their three million acres being even sparsely populated by the roughly three thousand Indians. While all three tribes had a stake in what happened to the grass, as the Comanches were located closer to the Red River than the other two tribes, they inevitably were impacted more by the neighboring Texas ranchers.

But not only herds bound for market constituted a problem. The beef contractors for the agency supplied animals from herds they were permitted to maintain on the reservation. Before long a contractor was being charged with holding many more cattle than were necessary to meet his commitment to the agency, the pick of the herd being driven to Kansas to sell after fattening on Indian grass.

Government employees, including Agent P. B. Hunt, tried to capitalize on the opportunities. Hunt asked permission to run a few cows, pledging, "I will not interfere with any Indian grazing ground, as there are thousands of acres of excellent grass going to waste." Squaw men and local traders also quickly recognized the possibilities of easy profits. The secretary of the interior summarily denied requests of traders and agency employees for grazing permits. Those whites, however, who might have acquired Indian wives, brought in cattle under their spouses' names or attempted to graze other men's herds, pocketing whatever the market would bear.

Fairly early another problem emerged in the form of Texas cattle that were permitted to drift across the Red River. After the spring runoff the river posed no real barrier, and agency officials began to complain that ranchers were deliberately holding cattle near the river knowing that they would be attracted to the north bank by its luxuriant grasses.

Army officers and agency officials never found a good solution to the problem of intruding cattle. A federal law authorized a tax of $1.00 per head on herds transiting reservations. First the herds must be located, however, and this could be done only by maintaining patrols in the western uninhabited area of the reservation. In the years following the Red River War, the size of the Fort Sill garrison was reduced to the point that it was impossible to monitor adequately the herds being trailed north, much less those drifting or being driven across the Red River. The inauguration in 1878 of a reservation police force helped a little, although its force was so small (only about two dozen) that few were available for that task. Moreover, even if an official identified transiting herds, he must make a complaint to a United States attorney and let him take action. If the process dragged out long enough, the herd owner could pay the tax and still profit handsomely from the additional weight his cattle would have gained. One enterprising cavalry officer simply took twenty-four cattle from herds moving north in June 1879 and turned them over to Kiowas and Kiowa-Apaches, whom he described as "half starving."

The Indians themselves quickly learned to make their own demands and, if these were refused, to stampede herds and run off what they needed. One Texas outfit reported losing 295 head in this fashion. In a more typical situation Indians would approach escorting cowboys and ask for a few steers. The trail boss usually complied, accepting this levy as simply a cost of using the trail across the reservation.

By 1881, however, transiting herds became the lesser of the evils. A bad drought that year led Texas ranchers to drive cattle in the thousands across the Red River with every intention of remaining as long as possible. To this end they began to make formal proposals to lease reservation land, as well as informal deals with influential Indians, usually Comanches, as the Kiowas and Kiowa-Apaches were too far away from the Red River to need to be bought off.

The first lease proposal to receive serious consideration was one made in late 1879 by the two men who held the beef contract. Quanah, not yet a convert to leasing, was a participant in a council of seventy-five Indians who discussed the issue with Agent Hunt. The Indians selected Horse Back, a Noconi Comanche, as their principal spokesman. Quanah, together with Stumbling Bear, a Kiowa, and White Man, an Apache, joined Horse Back in voicing Indian objections. The agent stated that he agreed with their refusal to lease pasture to the beef contractors, adding that if he could not get soldiers to drive off intruding cattle, he himself would do the job with the help of Indians, "Quinah [sic] and his men, for instance."

The Indians took the opportunity to raise other issues, Quanah reminding Hunt that only three weeks earlier he had been at the agency with Tabananaka, the Yamparika band chief, Cheevers, and White Wolf to question the location of the reservation's western boundary. What was at stake was the area to be defined for many years as Greer County, about 1,500,000 acres between the North Fork of the Red River and the hundredth meridian, the eastern boundary of the Texas Panhandle. Texas claimed the area and in 1860 had organized it as Greer County. Not until 1896 did the United States Supreme Court end the controversy by ruling against Texas and assigning Greer County to the public domain. Ultimately it became part of the state of Oklahoma. In 1884, however, Quanah was insisting that Greer County was really a part of the Indian reservation. For the next decade a few settlers established farms and ranches in the disputed area, crossed into the reservation to steal timber, and permitted their cattle to drift east, joining thousands of others eating Indian grass.

In June 1881 Quanah participated in another council relating to reservation use, and this time he spoke first and longest, although two other Comanches—Esahabbe, the Penateka chief, and Howeah, a Yamparika—also were heard. Quanah referred to the council at Medicine Lodge in 1867, "when I was a small boy," and the rights it guaranteed the Indians. He insisted that the cattle trails through the reservation be closed and that the efforts to make the Indians take private property in land be stopped. "All red people are as one in regard to this and wish to hold their country in common," the interpreter quoted him as declaring. Quanah also expressed Comanche discontent with the transfer of their agency to Anadarko and asked that an agent and associated services—trader, physician, blacksmith, and commissary—be located in the Comanche part of the reservation. Ever the diplomat, he took some of the edge off his demands by interjecting: "I am related to both the white and the red people. I realize it as so, and for that reason will not do anything bad, but looking for the good road, a suppliant for the red people, so when Washington hears he will help us."

Quanah's initial opposition to white men's cattle on the reservation began to change. He still, nevertheless, could not accept the government's dictate that the Indians could not completely block cattlemen's routes to market, although they might levy tolls for passage. He also drew a distinction between the ranchers, principally Texans, with whom he had had dealings over a period of years, and strangers using the reservation as a cattle trail or highway between Texas and Kansas. While Quanah reported Kiowas to the agent for seizing cattle from herds headed north and for threatening and hitting cowboys with their guns, he obtained a paper from the agent that enabled him to practice a similar form of blackmail. He would show this paper, which identified him as a Comanche chief, and, after offering advice on the best route to follow to have good grass and water, would request a few head for himself and his people. Quanah argued that he asked only for the lame cattle that would never make it to the railroad anyway, although the trail boss confronted by several armed and painted warriors would feel under some pressure to accomodate them.

If tough trail bosses were susceptible to such treatment, it is not surprising that it also was effective on ordinary travelers. Within the space of a few days in June 1889, two small parties on the road between Greer County and Fort Sill reported being forced by Quanah and some of his band to pay to go farther. It cost one group $6.00, and the other, apparently short of cash, $1.90 plus fifteen pounds of flour, six pounds of bacon, and some syrup. Of them Quanah had demanded $1.00 per wagon and $.10 per head of stock. This type of thing was not done on a regular basis, but it could have been a frightening and expensive experience for those travelers intercepted. Agency officials would try to respond to the complaints, although those were trivial matters when compared with other issues demanding their attention, like the question of leasing a million acres at annual rentals of thousands of dollars.

By the time the first major lease had been negotiated in December 1884, everyone involved recognized Quanah as the leader of the proleasing faction. His complete conversion to the cause can be traced to his mutually profitable associations with certain ranchers. These quickly learned that their best hope of avoiding continual friction with the local tribesmen, which could result in unacceptable losses of cattle or, worst of all, the Indians' burning the range, was to cultivate special relationships with chiefs and headmen. These Indian leaders would then use their influence to facilitate the rancher's access to the reservation and discourage thefts from his herd and those terrible fires that could destroy many square miles of pasturage.

Quanah developed a special relationship with the Harrold & Ikard outfit headquartered in Illinois. Early in 1883 it had sixty thousand cattle that, although nominally in Greer County, were spilling over the boundary of the reservation. On the recommendation of Horace P. Jones, the interpreter, not only did Harrold & Ikard employ Quanah and three others of his band, but over a period of eighteen months they gave the Indians about three hundred head of cattle. Presumably these would have been turned over to Quanah to distribute, thereby permitting him to strengthen his position by rewarding his supporters as well as building up his own herd. In the same fashion, George W. Fox, Jr., a former agency employee trying to make it as a cattleman, hired Eschiti and Esahabbe, while Samuel Burk Burnett and Daniel W. Waggoner, both Texas ranchers and later great and good friends of Quanah, had Permamsu (Afraid of Hair/Comanche Jack), a Yamparika, on their payroll.

A year later Colonel B. B. Groom, representative of the Francklyn Land & Cattle Company, which had bought out Harrold & Ikard's operation in Greer County, was employing Quanah and four unnamed Comanches. Quanah drew $50 a month, while the other four were paid $25, or approximately the same as cowboys. It is unlikely that any of them, and certainly not Quanah, was subjected to the harsh regimen that was a cowboy's lot. What the cattlemen were buying was their influence, as when Quanah accompanied Harrold & Ikard men dispatched to recover some of their stock from a Comanche. The Indian was absent when they arrived, and the cowboys drove off a dozen head, confident that Quanah's presence would prevent retaliation. His cooperation would be of much greater importance in the prolonged efforts to negotiate leases.

It required most of 1883 and 1884 for the Indians and the ranchers to reach agreement on lease terms. There were many complicating factors, not the least of which was the secretary of the interior's decision, based on rulings from the Justice Department, to exercise minimum control of the process. In this fashion the secretary hoped to avoid taking action that might be interpreted as contrary to treaties or infringing upon the rights of Congress.

Given the large number of applicants for leases—at one time thirty-five seeking a total of over twelve million acres when less than two million were available—any decision would leave a lot of unhappy people. The successful applicants would be those who were able to secure Indian backing, since the government was leaving so much in their hands. Two other groups also needing to be courted were agency officials and squaw men. Agency personnel were important because, although officials in Washington were refusing to play an active role in the negotiations, they still retained a veto power and would be influenced by reports from the scene. The squaw men, for their part, because of their intermarried status could sway tribal opinion.

The ultimately successful bargaining group had its allies among all three groups: Indians, agency personnel, and squaw men. Quanah was their principal Indian contact. Colonel Groom, who took the lead for the winners, referred to the Comanche as "admitted to be the most influential and brave man in the three tribes" and promised him five hundred head of cattle if his own company got access to 600,000 acres. Both Indian Agent P. B. Hunt and H. Kuhn, his chief clerk, were cooperating with Groom's group of applicants. The Francklyn Land & Cattle Company's man described Agent Hunt as "our fast fixed friend," suggesting some financial arrangement with him. That E. C. Suggs, one of the combine headed by Groom, had underwritten the $75,000 bond the government required of the Indian agent also helped keep Hunt in line. To ensure the cooperation of interpreter Thomas Woodard and W. H. Conover, a squaw man "smart and anxious to make money," Groom was prepared to meet their demands. Conover's price was a pasture large enough to run five thousand cattle, and Woodard wanted "about $1,000, 25 or 30 cattle and a small tract of land."

Throughout 1884 the membership of the "ring," as one investigator from Washington dubbed it, fluctuated as cattlemen joined it or dropped out. There were disagreements about tactics and how the range would be divided if they were successful. Financial problems finally forced Colonel Groom's company to pull out, after his heavy investment of time and energy had helped make the long-sought prize a reality.

The Indian alliances on the issue also shifted at times, although the leasing and antileasing nuclei remained firm. The Comanches generally supported leasing, while most Kiowas opposed it. The antileasing faction, in communications to officials and in councils on the reservation and in Washington, made clear the basis of their opposition. They felt that their future as farmers and stockmen would be endangered by turning over half of the reservation to the white men. Not only would it restrict the area open to the Indians, but the income from the lease, the so-called grass money, would encourage gambling among their young men and distract them from opening farms and caring for their own livestock. Such arguments had a "progressive" ring to them that should have placed their articulators clearly in that camp, although the lines of demarcation between the progressives and the traditionalists were never clear-cut, as Quanah's own career demonstrates.

Quanah was a favorite target of the antileasers, being repeatedly denounced by them. Tabananaka and White Wolf were prominent among the Comanche opponents of leasing. Like Quanah, Tabananaka was showing the way for other Comanches by building a cattle herd of his own. Nevertheless, he joined White Wolf, a fellow Yamparika, in denouncing Quanah as "bought by the cattlemen, and don't come and talk with the rest of us chiefs." They declared that the Quahadas as a division were "unsettled . . . want to run around all the time . . . don't farm" and criticized them for not sending their children to school. On other occasions the antileasers dismissed Quanah as a "half-breed" backed by a minority, and even called for his replacement as chief by Howeah, a Yamparika. This was proposed at a council with the agent, the transcript of which was signed by thirty-seven Comanches. They included not only Tabananaka and White Wolf, but Horse Back, Cheevers, and Mow-way (Shaking Hand), a Kotsateka, all prominent chiefs. Horse Back was the Noconi to whose band the agent had assigned Quanah when he came in from the plains in 1875.

Despite the criticism, Quanah and his proleasing allies made a strong case in the fifteen-odd months that the controversy raged. Their principal argument was that the grass was going to waste, or being consumed by the cattle of ranchers who were paying little if anything for the privilege. With the help of agency chief clerk H. Kuhn, who apparently was working for Colonel Groom, Quanah composed a formal statement to Agent Hunt justifying leasing because "we are poor and in our present condition are unable to use these lands ourselves, and, we hope by these means to . . . secure the money with which to stock our lands, and . . . enable us to become self-supporting." Obviously both sides in this debate strove to present themselves as seeking to become independent of government support. The antileasers would appear to have had the best of that argument as they sought to substantiate Indian need for the entire reservation for farms and pasture.

What the antileasers lacked, however, was the support of a group of enterprising and politically adept whites like that headed by Colonel Groom, and an Indian leader with the energy, personality, and celebrity of Quanah. It was no coincidence that Quanah's name appeared on virtually all of the communications of the proleasing group, usually heading the list if there was more than one signator. Even when he was unable to be present at a council, Quanah's name and prestige were invoked by his people. As Permamsu phrased it on one such occasion: "All you see here are Quanah's men and have Quanah's talk. . . . Quanah is way off. . . . The talk we will give you Quanah knows; he has heard the talk."

In August 1884 the Comanche chief appeared in Washington on his first of many visits to the nation's capital. Subsidized by the cattlemen interested in leasing, the party also included Quanah's lieutenant Permamsu and four other Indians, three of them Kiowas. They were accompanied by Philip McCusker, interpreter for the all-important 1867 Treaty of Medicine Lodge and later employed on the Indian agency staff and at Fort Sill. An investigator from Washington believed that in 1884 McCusker was functioning as much like an attorney as an interpreter.

The Comanches and Kiowas had meetings with the heads of the Interior Department and the Office of Indian Affairs while in Washington. Members of the delegation later quoted the officials as deploring the lack of Indian unity on the leasing question but refusing to intervene. Unfortunately, no transcripts of Quanah's first exchanges with officials in Washington have been uncovered.

As the leasing issue approached resolution late in 1884, Quanah was in the thick of the action. In October he reported to the agent on a meeting he had attended at Wichita Falls, Texas, called by George Fox, who offered $3,000 for grazing privileges. The tribesmen refused the money, but Quanah observed that Fox already was running two thousand head on the reservation under the protection of Eschiti's band. Another white man, J. P. Addington, had established a camp only ten miles from Fort Sill, in the general area Quanah's band occupied. The cattlemen now controlled a broad crescent running along the southern and western borders of the reservation. The antileasers may have had principle on their side, but in the real world of the 1880s probably the most that could be done was for the tribes to make the best deal possible with the men whose herds were consuming their grass.

For the leasers, nonleasers, and cattlemen, November and December brought a flurry of meetings. Commissioner of Indian Affairs Hiram Price sent Special Agent Paris H. Folsom to monitor the bargaining process, and Folsom labored mightily to identify the various interest groups involved. Although no stranger to reservation skulduggery, the special agent was moved at one point by the machinations of the cattlemen, agency personnel, and squaw men to comment to his superior, with no apologies to Bret Harte: "For ways that are dark and tricks that are vain, the white man beats the Indian." It is difficult, however, to envision Cynthia Ann's son as just another Indian dupe.

By now Quanah was gaining recognition among his fellow Comanches as the principal chief of their tribe. There was no precedent for this, nevertheless, the office being discussed when his opponents plotted to replace Quanah, a Quahada, with Howeah, a Yamparika, was that of tribal chief. When the Comanches roamed the plains in bands, there could be no real tribal government. Reservation conditions were forcing the Indians to recognize the need for more centralized tribal authority. The progress toward that goal would be agonizingly slow as division, band, and family loyalties held firm for many years. Meanwhile, each side on the leasing issue would try to convince the government that it represented a majority on the reservation.

In mid-November Quanah, with the aid of a Texas cattleman as scribe, informed Special Agent Folsom that the tribes had conferred and that a majority favored leasing. The Comanche also made it clear that the Indians wanted the lease money paid directly to them rather than deposited in the United States Treasury to be doled out as Washington determined. Quanah was concerned that there might be a mingling of government and Indian funds and some impairment of the government's commitment under the 1867 treaty "to furnish us rations and annuities for thirty years." In one significant respect Quanah was in error, although he was voicing a commonly held Indian view. The treaty contained no provision for rations. To wean the Indians from the life of the hunt, the government had provided rations when they took up residence on the reservation, although that had been perceived by officials as only a temporary expedient, not the beginning of a thirty-year dole.

Quanah's claim that the proleasing element represented a majority of the Comanches, Kiowas, and Kiowa-Apaches conflicted with Special Agent Folsom's own poll. He concluded that it was the antileasing element that enjoyed a clear majority, 402 to 290. And this was despite Quanah's having recruited some Penatekas, although bands of that division had been attached to the Wichita Agency for several years. Thus it was a surprise to at least Folsom when on December 23 a lease agreement was drawn up that 404 Comanches, Kiowas, and Kiowa-Apaches signed. Testifying to the authenticity of signatures on the document and to its having been accurately interpreted to the Indians were four white men, all of whom were in some fashion interested parties. For example, Emmet Cox was an employee of a cattleman and the husband of a daughter of Yamparika Chief Quirts Quip (and a future son-in-law of Quanah). E. L. Clark was also a prominent squaw man, and the only intermarried white listed as one of the parties to the lease. R. P. Sanders, the interpreter for the council that produced the lease, was also known to be in the employ of the cattlemen. Nine individuals or companies were listed as leasers, including George W. Fox, Jr., Samuel Burk Burnett, and E. C. Suggs & Bro.

Despite the possible conflicts of interest and the remarkable turnabout in the voting, Agent Hunt hastened to endorse the lease. It had been presented to him by a delegation headed by Quanah Parker, who was now beginning to insist on the inclusion of his adopted surname. The agent described the terms as the best for the Indians of any yet negotiated and "fairly in their interest." The Indians would receive annually six cents per acre for the six-year life of the lease. In addition the leasers pledged to employ fifty-four tribesmen at wages of $35 per month for the chiefs and $20 for their followers. Hunt pointed out that the area being leased "has never in any way been used by the Indians, but to a great extent has been depredated upon by trespassers and the most of it is unsuitable for farming." He declared the leasers were "known to me to be reliable and responsible" and vouched for the agreement having the support of a majority of the Indian adults. Hunt was on his way out of office, having resigned under pressure, but he had earned whatever the cattlemen had paid him. He would next be heard of running a herd on the reservation, probably on pasture allotted him by the leasing combine.

Quanah's services to the cattlemen continued uninterrupted. Early in February 1885 he appeared in Washington accompanied by two other Comanches, Saddy-teth-ka (Dog Eater), faithful Permamsu, and by Loud Talker, a Kiowa. Leasers George Fox and E. C. Suggs, with Horace Jones the interpreter, escorted the Indian delegation. Former agent James M. Haworth, now superintendent of Indian schools, sat in on their conference with Secretary of the Interior Henry M. Teller. The delegation's object was to ensure that Secretary Teller had not been swayed by an antileasing delegation headed by Tabananaka that had been in Washington in January.

Quanah, referred to in the official transcript as "Quanah Parker, chief of the Comanches," was interrogated first by Secretary Teller.

When asked about the objections of the antileasing group, Quanah dismissed his opponents summarily: "I cannot tell what objection they have to it, unless they have not got sense. They are kind of old fogy, on the wild road yet, unless they have not got brains enough to sabe [*sic*] the advantage there is in it."

In response to other questions by the secretary, Quanah explained why he selected this particular group from among the large pool of applicants for leases: "for the reason that they have lived right on the border here for a number of years, and I know them and they have treated me well, and that is the reason I made the lease to these parties." When the secretary asked whether he had been compensated in any fashion by the cattlemen, Quanah responded with a catagorical denial, "They have not paid me anything for the lease." This statement can most charitably be described as a half-truth.

After having heard Permamsu support Quanah's version of the affair, Secretary Teller tacitly approved the lease. Although declaring that, "I cannot say anything about the lease, because Congress has all this question . . . before them," he did say, "I think this is a very good lease if they have reserved as much land as they want for their own farming and cattle purposes." Quanah had at least allayed the secretary's worst fears with his statement that "there is enough left for all horses and cattle, and we were very particular in making the lease not to lease any land that came within the neighborhood of any of our farm settlements."

The leases were of considerable consequence for the Comanches and for Quanah personally. They inflicted on the tribe new factions as Indians lined up for and against the deal, and they also to some extent pitted the Comanches and the Kiowas against each other. Nevertheless, it was never a strictly intertribal dispute. For a time there were both Kiowas and Comanches who refused to accept their grass money, the semiannual payments amounting to about $10 per person.

Quanah was a clear winner from the protracted negotiations. The whites, and some of the Indians, now accepted him as the premier spokesman for the reservation's Indian population. He had demonstrated that, as he had phrased it in the interview with Secretary Teller, "I am somewhat acquainted with the ways of the white people." Quanah was learning what the whites wanted, and where that agreed with his own interests and those of his people as he saw them, he was happy to cooperate.

That Quanah profited in the material sense is also clear. He continued on the payroll of the cattlemen, drawing at a minimum the $35 per month the lease guaranteed some chiefs. In view of Colonel Groom's promise to him of five hundred head of cattle, it can be

assumed that the leasers contributed substantially to the size of his
herd. Finally, as some opposition to the lease persisted and there
were threats to burn pastures and the inevitable disputes over fences
being cut and stock stolen, it was in the interest of the cattlemen to
keep Quanah loyal by gifts and by junkets to Dallas and Fort Worth.
Not that the Comanche chief enjoyed this largesse alone. Comanche
custom required their leaders to share their material goods; visitors
to Quanah's home place were always struck by the number of Indians
camped in the vicinity and beneficiaries of his bounty.

Quanah had come a long way in the ten years since he had arrived
at Fort Sill to surrender to the military authorities. The status of a
rising young warrior was then the most he could claim among his
fellow Comanches, although his mixed-blood ancestry had made him
a curiosity to the white men in a position to facilitate his advancement.
By 1885 he was enjoying growing recognition among the whites, and
even some of his fellow Comanches, as the tribe's leading chief.

CHAPTER 4

Following the White Man's Road

FOLLOWING the signing of the first grazing leases in late 1884, Quanah worked to consolidate his position as the principal Comanche chief. Along the way he opened a farm and built a house that any white man in the area would have been happy to own, served as a judge of the agency's Court of Indian Offenses, and presided over a growing family. His ties to Texas cattlemen remained close as he served as their contact with the reservation population and espoused their cause with government officials.

Quanah recognized that to advance in his new situation he needed to court the agent. That individual had it in his power either to aid and abet or to put obstacles in the path of an ambitious Indian. Quanah sought to assure each of the several agents in this period of his loyalty and support. Although the writing styles of those who penned his letters varied widely in spelling and syntax, his concern for the approval of his agents, bordering on obsequiousness, is apparent. Typical is a letter, transcribed by someone of limited education, to P. B. Hunt shortly before that agent left office. In it Quanah avowed his loyalty: "Even though I am here with my friends yet their [*sic*] is but one council I listen to, and that is yours, and the same way with the Indians. I do not listen to any foolish talks. I wait and listen to you alone you are my agent." Several years later, with the help of a more competent writer, Quanah recalled the advice he had received from Colonel Mackenzie and Agent Haworth when he reported in to Fort Sill: "Follow the white man's path." Quanah insisted he had done so: "Upon all occasions I have assisted and carried out the views and wishes of those mentioned [agents and army officers] so far as I was able." And indeed he had.

Not content to advertise his own virtues, Quanah was never reluctant to bring to the attention of officials the shortcomings of his opponents in reservation politics. At this time they consisted of the

Kiowas as a tribe and his fellow Comanche, Tabananaka. The latter had earned Quanah's ire by opposing leasing and by deriding Quanah in remarks to officials. In turn, Quanah accused him of being a reactionary and of harassing Quanah's white farmhands. The Comanche chief charged the Kiowas with trying to block the grass leases and generally contributing to unrest on the reservation. In the 1880s the Kiowas produced at least three prophets who preached against the Indians trying to travel the white man's road. Unlike the Comanches, the Kiowas were strongly attached to their annual Sun Dance, despite the disapproval of agency officials and the increasing difficulty of obtaining the proper paraphernalia and setting for their religious ceremonies. In 1887 they had been forced to purchase from Texas rancher Charles Goodnight a buffalo to obtain the required hide to crown the center pole of the Sun Dance lodge that year.

As the Kiowas began preparations for their Sun Dance in the spring of 1887, they had been further emboldened by the message of a new prophet, Pa-ingya. He promised supernatural assistance in the form of a violent windstorm and prairie fire that would destroy the whites and the agency buildings, including the school at Anadarko. The Indians could escape this catastrophe by discarding white man's clothes and weapons and by removing their children from the doomed school. The Kiowas were divided in their reception of Pa-ingya's message. His decision to assemble his followers at a camp near Lone Wolf's indicated that the Kiowa chief and old political rival of Quanah's had not rejected the prophet.

Agent J. Lee Hall, P. B. Hunt's successor, appealed to the commandant of Fort Sill for troop backup because of the Kiowa threat. Hunt repeated his request on receiving a warning from Quanah. The Comanche reminded the agent of his being asked to keep an eye on Kiowa medicine making and revealed that Kiowas had approached him for help in assaulting Fort Sill that summer. Quanah tried to reassure the agent, "Me and my people have quit fighting long ago," but his message only further alarmed Lee Hall. The agent passed a copy of Quanah's letter on to Fort Sill, whose commanding officer included it as a communication from "a prominent Comanche" in his report to the adjutant general on troop movements. These actions, together with the intercession of an educated Kiowa convert to Christianity, Joshua Given, undercut Pa-ingya's support among the Kiowas. But not before newspaper accounts appearing nationwide had carried stories about Kiowa unrest, and one spoke of the role of the "half-breed chief, Quanah Parker." This particular story had been datelined Quanah, Texas, the railroad town in North Texas named in honor of Cynthia Ann's son, and had been reprinted in the *New York Times*. Other papers carried a story from Fort Worth that credited Quanah with the peaceful outcome: he "not only held his own tribe in check, but influenced the better element of Kiowas." Paingya was discredited by the failure of his medicine while Quanah's standing with the agency and Fort Sill personnel rose as he received his first notice in the national press.

Quanah had received even more attention as the result of the publication in Texas the previous year of a brief biography of his mother. The author, James T. DeShields, had obtained from Agent Hall a photograph of Quanah for his book. Apparently DeShields did not go to Fort Sill to interview the Comanche personally, although his volume included flattering comments about him: "Quanah speaks English, is considerably advanced in civilization, and owns a ranch with considerable livestock and a small farm; wears a citizen's suit and conforms to the customs of civilization—withal a fine-looking and dignified son of the plains." DeShields also referred to a letter Quanah had written to the *Fort Worth Gazette* seeking a picture of his mother. His letter inspired Sul Ross, who had commanded the detachment that had captured Cynthia Ann, to send Quanah a copy of a daguerreotype made when she visited Fort Worth in 1862.

As DeShields had reported, Quanah was becoming a cattleman on a small scale. Over the years he had built his herd from government distribution of foundation stock and gifts from his friends and employers among the Texas ranchers. These included men who ran no cattle on the reservation, like Charles Goodnight, who had given him some stock, including "a good Durham bull" to improve his breed. The government tried to encourage the Indians by buying animals from them to help make up the beef issue, and Quanah took advantage of this. In August 1884, for example, he offered to the agent at least forty head of three- and four-year-olds which could have brought him as much as $400.

Quanah also pleased the agents by venturing into farming, although officials at Anadarko recognized that cattle were a better bet than crops for the Indians of this reservation. The Comanche chief did not plant and harvest himself; rather, he relegated these laborious tasks to a young white sharecropper, David A. Grantham, and additional white farmhands as needed. Special Agent E. E. White, who had replaced Lee Hall when the latter was charged with fraud, stated in 1888 that Quanah was farming 150 acres and characterized him as "broad, liberal, and progressive." Two years later agency reports depicted Quanah's farm as a flourishing operation with 425 cattle and 200 hogs, three wagons and one buggy. He also had 160 horses, a clue that he still measured wealth, at least in part, as Comanches had for as long as they could remember. Despite the large herd of horses, Agent Charles E. Adams, a grocer from Maryland whose good Republican connections had won him the appointment at Anadarko, considered Quanah "a particularly progressive Indian." Agent Adams also was sympathetic to the Comanche's request for government assistance in building a house.

Quanah first considered such a project in 1882, although it would be nearly ten years before he traded his tepee for a frame home. His first proposal was for a simple two-room structure estimated to cost no more than $350, one typical of scores built for Indians on the reservation in the 1880s. He apparently had second thoughts about giving up camp life, and for the next eight years was happy with his tepee, supplemented by the traditional brush arbor in the summer. By 1890, however, camp life was no longer acceptable for the man claiming to be the "Principal Chief of the Comanche Indians," as his letterhead stationery proclaimed him. Before getting a promise of government support, Quanah purchased $1,000 worth of lumber and contracted to have a two-story, ten-room house built. It would be two years before he moved in, as carpenters came and went and additions were made, such as a 10' × 10' one-story structure and an impressive porch. Even before the additions, Quanah estimated his house had cost $2,000 to build.

Over a period of two years the Comanche made repeated efforts to get government help in constructing his house. His tenant David Grantham, who was living in a dugout, approached the agent on the subject, telling him that Quanah wanted to be subsidized at least partially and that if the government was not forthcoming, "he will see the stock men and get the money." Agent Adams applied to Washington for $500 for Quanah, arguing that "he is an Indian who deserves some assistance from the Government." When that appeal was ignored, Adams repeated it, assuring the commissioner of Indian affairs that Quanah intended to "go into camp no more." Commissioner T. J. Morgan, a fervent Baptist and staunch advocate of "civilizing" the Indians, reminded Adams: "While at your agency I stated to you personally that I did not deem it wise for the government to contribute money to assist in building a house for an Indian who has five wives. I do not think the proposition admits of discussion."

But that did not end the matter, as both Quanah and Agent Adams filed additional requests in Washington. The Comanche even tried appealing over Commissioner Morgan's head to the secretary of the interior. In a letter drafted by someone with writing skills superior to those of the semiliterate Grantham, Quanah argued that other Indians had received government help "when it was known that they had a plurality of wives, and it did not militate against them." He indicated, furthermore, that he felt he was being discriminated against for something that had been "the custom of our people from time immemorial." Although ten white men, including the commandant of Fort Sill and Agent Adams, added a statement praising Quanah, it was to no avail. The secretary referred the matter back to Commissioner Morgan, who remained adamant: "As it is against the policy of this office to encourage or in any way countenance polygamy, no assistance will be granted Parker in the erection of his house, unless he will agree, in writing, to make a choice among his wives and to live only with the one chose and to fully provide for his other wives without living with them."

Six months later while in Washington, Quanah made one last effort in a note to the secretary of the interior. This time he pointed out that the 1867 treaty had provided $750 for a house for Toshaway (Silver Brooch), who had been the leading Penateka chief, although certainly not recognized as the principal chief of the Comanche Indians. Nevertheless, Quanah argued that as the house had not been built for Toshaway (he was wrong there), the $750 should be assigned to him. Again the Indian commissioner responded for the secretary, maintaining that agency records indicated that the $750 had been expended and the treaty provision satisfied. Quanah may have had too many wives to get money from the government, but the cattlemen who had a stake in keeping him happy made substantial contributions to his building fund.

Quanah's complicated marital situation also adversely affected his tenure as the leading judge on the agency's Court of Indian Offenses. Secretary of the Interior Henry M. Teller had launched the courts because of his unhappiness with certain aspects of reservation life such as the prevalence of "heathenish dances," polygamy, and medicine men. Responding in 1883 to his superior's concern, the commissioner of Indian affairs drafted the first regulations for a system of courts. Each was to be manned by three Indian judges, who could levy fines up to $100 and hand down prison sentences not to exceed six months. In the next ten years courts appeared at most agencies. While their performances varied widely, the judges did help to maintain order and to bridge the gulf between the cultures.

Eight years before a Court of Indian Offenses was instituted for the combined Kiowa, Comanche, and Wichita Agency, Quanah had complained about Indian witnesses having to go all the way to Fort Smith, Arkansas, to help prosecute horse thieves: "We want to know why the cases cannot be tried here." When the court was organized by Agent Hall in 1886, he chose Quanah as one of the first judges to serve. Except for brief intervals he continued in office until 1898, during most of that time carrying the designation of "presiding judge."

As the pay never exceeded $12 per month and the duty involved passing judgment on one's fellow tribesmen (Lone Wolf would resign from the court because of Kiowa opposition to his serving), Quanah could have accepted appointment only because of the status afforded him. He was never content to serve in the rear ranks; if there were honors to be distributed, he must get the lion's share.

Just how important a role the judges would play depended upon the whim of the agent. Only he could summon the court into session and assign it cases. Agent Hall initiated the court's career at the Kiowa, Comanche, and Wichita Agency, but almost immediately he permitted it to lapse. Quanah prodded Hall's successor, E. E. White, to revive the court. A Comanche had shot a Mexican captive, and Quanah thought that "we should call the Indian Court together and determine what should be done." Within a few weeks Agent White responded by appointing as judges Quanah, Lone Wolf, and a Wichita, Tehuacana Jim. The agent referred to them as "men of intelligence and integrity" and proposed, in vain, that the presiding judge, Quanah, be paid $30 per month and his associates $25, all three to receive extra rations while serving.

Agent W. D. Myers followed White and served only thirteen months before being replaced for political reasons. He also saw fit to employ the court. Myers reported that the two reservations that composed his agency were relatively crime-free, although he had referred some property disputes to the court. Myers testified that "settlement was had to the satisfaction, apparently, of all parties concerned."

The degree of complexity of some of these property cases can be seen in one in 1891 involving inheritance rights in the estate of Che-wa-wa, deceased. A cast-off wife claimed widow's rights and was contending with a brother for some horses that had belonged to Che-wa-wa. The court heard from the widow that the horses were all the offspring of a mare that had been purchased with Mexican blankets acquired in exchange for eight buffalo robes. According to the brother, however, the deceased had purchased the mare with income from the sale of three black-tailed deer skins and that, moreover, the deceased had promised him the horses if he died. The court ruled for the widow, although they left no opinion explaining their decision.

A few months later the court had to deal with charges of theft of livestock, manslaughter, and bigamy. The horse thief was ordered to return the animal or pay the owner $40. If he did neither, he would go to jail. Two Indians charged with stealing a yearling worth $8 were fined $10 each. The man accused of manslaughter was found guilty, but since the judges accepted his explanation that he thought that he had been pointing an unloaded pistol, he was sentenced to only ten days in jail. The Indian with marital problems was found guilty and given the option of going to jail or giving his first wife, whom he had cast off, a "well broken" pony and $10 cash.

Quanah and his fellow judges dispensed a justice that was an amalgam of traditional practices and American jurisprudence. Comanche justice tended to stress compensating the victim, as opposed to American law's concern with punishing the criminal. And while the judges, regardless of their mandate, proved reluctant to move against native religious customs, they were more willing to interfere with inheritance practices which favored the man's brothers at the expense of his widow.

As early as 1890 Quanah's own marital problems had attracted the attention of an inspector from Washington. He informed the secretary of the interior, who shared the information with Indian Commissioner Morgan, that Quanah, while "trying to walk in the white man's ways, and is in some respects in advance of his people in that direction," nevertheless had five wives. This raised serious questions about his real commitment to government policy. Commissioner Morgan did his own checking and concluded that the situation was even worse, that Quanah really had six wives and was wooing a seventh. Morgan therefore directed Agent Charles E. Adams to remove Quanah from the bench, deny him rations, and relieve him of his chieftainship.

Agent Adams did not wish to lose the services of a chief who was so generally cooperative, and thus he temporized. He promised to conduct a thorough investigation and report later. When he did, Adams admitted Quanah's "much married condition" and acknowledged that his "wives are five undisputed facts." The agent, however, did his best to persuade Commissioner Morgan of a set of unusual circumstances:

> Quanah has, with few exceptions, thrown his influence with the Agents, taking issue against the Kiowas at one time when they threatened Agent Hall, and proving in many ways that he was desirous of walking on "Washington's" road. He is ambitious and shrewd enough to know that any real progress for himself and his people must be by the white man's way; consequently he can recognize authority and see the wisdom of sometimes combatting the customs and prejudices of his people. . . .
>
> If Quanah is ineligible, any other Comanche whom I select would be ineligible for the same reason; the men of influence being, without exception, men of family.

Apparently Agent Adams made a good case, as Judge Parker survived that threat to remove him from the bench.

Four years later Quanah was in trouble once again. Indian Commissioner D. M. Browning had heard that he had taken another wife and ordered him to give her up or suffer removal from the Court of Indian Offenses. This was a particularly messy affair, as another Comanche, Eck-cap-ta, also claimed her. The woman, To-pay (Something Fell), wished to stay with Quanah, so he handed over the two horses, a carriage and harness, and $50 that Eck-cap-ta had set as his price. Nevertheless, Eck-cap-ta was unmollified and threatened To-pay. Quanah told his agent that "if he whip her or cut her ears off nooes [sic] off that I would whip him." Quanah acknowledged "my understanding that she is not to be either of our wife." He furthermore prepared a pledge dated August 23, 1894, committing himself to give up the woman: "This is to certify that I Quanah Parker principal chief of the Comanches have this day . . . give my word to the act. Indian Agent Lieut. Maury Nichols 7th U.S. Inf. that I give up and relinquish all claims to To-pay, as my wife & will immediately on my return to my home give her back to her people." But apparently it was true love, as To-pay remained with Quanah, bore him two children, and was one of his two wives when he died.

That he valued the judgeship as well as his wives is apparent in his reaction to changes in reservation governance by Lieutenant Maury Nichols in 1894. The second of the army officers to be detailed for duty to the agency as part of an effort to combat corruption and inefficiency in the Indian service, Nichols lasted less than a year before pleading ill health as a reason for seeking reassignment. During his brief tenure he had attempted to employ a new governance body in a way that Quanah regarded as an infringement on his authority as Comanche chief and on the jurisdiction of the Indian court.

Lieutenant Nichol's predecessor, an army officer who served only six months, had created a six-man committee for the Comanches, one that Quanah held had not been "independent of me or the Police Court, but worked with and under me, and the Court." What upset Quanah was that Lieutenant Nichols had changed the membership of the committee, appointing "blanket Indians who don't understand business . . . and this committee, instead of helping me and the other Judges, acts as an independent court, & this results in confusion." The lieutenant was forced to defend his action to the Indian commissioner, arguing that an open Comanche council had nominated the committee's members, but since they "are not the followers of Quanah . . . he considers it a stab at his authority and wants it disbanded." Within a week, however, Nichols was asking to be relieved of the agency responsibilities, so it did not become a real test of wills between him and the Comanche chief. As usual, where agents did not serve more than a year or two, they were unable to assert themselves against entrenched forces like squaw men, licensed traders, and chiefs with the energy, political skills, and ambition of Quanah.

Quanah's "much married condition" ultimately would be his undoing as the presiding judge of a court designed, among other things, to ban polygamy. In 1898 Commissioner of Indian Affairs William A. Jones ordered Captain Frank D. Baldwin, who had replaced Lieutenant Nichols as agent, to fire Quanah and Apiatan, a Kiowa judge, for being polygamists. Agent Baldwin did his best to save their positions. Commissioner Jones had selected replacements for them, and Baldwin denounced Jones's Comanche choice as "a tricky and deceitful man," guilty of taking bribes during a previous tour on the bench. The agent dismissed the commissioner's Kiowa nominee as "a worthless, good-for-nothing Indian." Baldwin's defense of Quanah was touching: "It is a matter of record that Quanah Parker when approached by the Commissioner on this point [polygamy] asked the Commissioner to select which one of his wives he should retain and which he should discard, at the same time stating that he had children by all of his wives, he loved them equally and loved his children and cared for them equally."

The agent also sought the intercession of H. L. Scott, who had been active in Indian affairs while stationed at Fort Sill. He told Scott that the Indians, in open council, had nominated Quanah and Apiatan to serve as judges. Baldwin also asked Scott to enlist the help of General Nelson A. Miles to defeat the machinations of a ring. The presumed conspirators included an attorney and sundry licensed traders and Interior Department personnel, and they were trying to get rid of anyone who stood in their way. Apparently Quanah and Apiatan had supported Agent Baldwin against the ring and now they would pay the price. Helping seal their fate was a petition signed by about one hundred of Quanah's fellow tribesmen, probably orchestrated by the ring. It called for his removal as chief because "he has worked against our welfare and interest and we have lost our confidence in him."

Nearly a century later it is difficult to get a clear fix on Quanah's "much married condition." When Commissioner Jones engineered the Comanche's dismissal from the court, Quanah still was listed by the agency as living with five wives. These five (in the order in which he had married them) were: Weck-e-ah (Hunting for Something), Cho-ny (Going with the Wind), Ma-cheet-to-wooky (Pushing Ahead), To-nar-cy (Straight), and To-pay (Something Fell). About this time some agency records recorded To-nar-cy as his wife, the other four being designated as "Mothers." To-nar-cy is sometimes described as his "show wife," the one who accompanied him on trips to Washington and elsewhere. She also is the only one who bore him no children, which may explain her availability for excursions. But Quanah was never at a loss for children, siring twenty-four by one count; five of them died in infancy, and sixteen survived him. Two other wives, A-er-wuth-takum (She Fell with a Wound) and Co-by (Standing with a Head), were no longer with Quanah in 1898. Which of the parties to the divorces had taken the initiative is unclear, although A-er-wuth-takum is identified in some agency records as a "discarded wife." Nor is there an obvious explanation for the identity of the Pop-e-ah-waddy, a "wife" who accompanied him to Washington in June 1890, and for whose travel expenses he unsuccessfully sought reimbursement. However, since it was in behalf of the cattlemen that he had gone to Washington and since they subsidized his travel, Quanah does not seem to have suffered any financial embarrassment from the outing.

Students of the Plains Indians usually portray them as having great difficulty in giving up their nomadic ways, and also as prepared at the slightest pretext to visit around their large reservations or to call on friends in neighboring tribes. Quanah certainly did not often turn down opportunities to travel. Between December 1884 and September 1892 he visited Washington four times. Quanah quickly adapted to train travel and hotel living. Years after the event, a Fort Sill post trader remembered dining in St. Louis with a delegation of Indians en route home from Washington. He recalled that the other Indians watched Quanah and followed his example as the seasoned traveler unfolded his napkin and arranged it across his lap.

Quanah also made several visits to Texas as guest of his friends the cattlemen, one outing almost resulting in his death. In December 1885 he was at Fort Worth with Yellow Bear, either the father of Quanah's second wife, Weck-e-ah, or her uncle (accounts vary). The two Comanches were sharing a room at the Pickwick Hotel. One evening an employee of rancher Daniel W. Waggoner took Quanah out on the town, "to search for a fair inamorata with whom he had been long acquainted," according to a Fort Worth reporter. Yellow Bear remained in the hotel, and Quanah returned hours later to find him asleep. Quanah lit a gas light long enough to prepare for bed but apparently did not completely turn it off when he retired. During the night both men awakened and rose before being overcome by the gas. Yellow Bear never recovered consciousness. Quanah was saved because he fell near a draft of fresh air. It was sufficient to keep him alive until the following afternoon, when the hotel clerk finally investigated their absence. Within two days Quanah had recovered enough so that Agent Lee Hall could get him and Yellow Bear's remains on a train and deliver them to Harrold, Texas, the nearest station to the reservation. News of Yellow Bear's death had been telegraphed ahead, and the train was met by a crowd of mourners, some of them displaying the traditional bleeding cuts and cropped hair of the bereaved Comanche. Quanah was sufficiently apprehensive about how the news of Yellow Bear's death might be received that he had obtained a copy of the coroner's inquest to forestall any wild rumors about the circumstances.

Besides his trips to Fort Worth and Washington, Quanah also made a few visits to New Mexico. One of these must have been in 1884, when a newspaper reporter in San Antonio had him headed for Mexico City. The reporter's description of Quanah's appearance was hopefully more accurate: "He wears a citizen's suit of black, neatly fitting, regular 'tooth-pick' dude shoes, a watch and gold chain and black felt hat." His hair was braided, and the two plaits were worn down his back. The following year he passed through Fort Worth in October, en route to New Mexico. His destination was the Mescalero Reservation, whose agent would report that Quanah had visited them for ten days and "given them much good advice and counsel. I regard Mr. Parker as a good man." Again in 1886 he was absent from the reservation for about two weeks, probably on another trip to New Mexico. His only other visit to the Mescalero Reservation for which there is documentation is one in 1892. It was the subject of a letter that Quanah wrote to the commissioner of Indian affairs. He reported having seen improvements in the Mescalero during the years he had been visiting them and was not reluctant to let his own light shine through: "I have talked to these Indians about making their own living, and, to live like white men. I keep my own people straight. It is what you want at Washington to keep the people straight."

As with so many other things involving Quanah, it is impossible to state conclusively why he was visiting the Mescalero. Certainly his first wife, To-ha-yea, had been Mescalero, and there is some speculation that he might even have lived with those people for a period. He justified one trip to his agent by asserting that he was seeking the return of some Comanches who had taken refuge there in the mid-1870s, including a sister. Either the agent misunderstood Quanah, or he was using a broader Comanche definition of sister, as there is no other evidence for her existence. A more likely explanation for Quanah's continued interest in the Mescalero was his sharing their attachment to peyote. Unaware of this, Agent Hall endorsed the visit to the Mescalero in 1885, assuring the Indian commissioner that Quanah was "a man of sterling integrity and of more influence and better standing than any other man among all the Indians in my charge."

The "Principal Chief of the Comanche Indians" had become an example of a type that Melissa Meyer has referred to as the "broker," and Loretta Fowler as the "political middleman." Agents were willing to accept intercession for the Indians from an economic progressive who had his own farm, ran several hundred head of cattle, and usually dressed like a white man except for his two braids. The agents would be even more forthcoming if this chief was as vocal as Quanah in support of the general objectives of United States Indian policy. Whether it was cattle or barbed wire, farm implements or rations, Quanah got his share. At the same time, however, he continued to represent his people to the government and to provide for the less fortunate, roles Comanches expected of their leaders. And in strictly social matters such as marriage and religion, Quanah balanced his economic progressivism with sufficient adherence to traditional practices to retain the respect of most Comanches. Sometimes this required a delicate balancing act, as when he inveighed publicly against the Ghost Dance while privately serving as the principal advocate for peyote on the two reservations of the agency. He was proving to be the very model of the broker or political middleman, with one foot on the white man's road and the other on the old Comanche trail.

CHAPTER 5

Peyote Advocate
and Ghost Dance Critic

IN 1890 Quanah and his fellow Indians at the Kiowa, Comanche, and Wichita Agency heard of Wovoka (Jack Wilson), a Paiute messiah who was promising to restore to the tribesmen a world they feared had been lost forever. By 1890 many Comanches already had become devotees of a religion featuring peyote and that was providing them some solace in those troubled times. The plant that they turned to for comfort and inspiration was a small spineless cactus whose closest habitat to the Comanches was in the lower Rio Grande Valley. Believers were interested only in the buttons, those parts of the peyote plant that appeared above ground, which Weston La Barre has described as looking like "a little dumpling or pincushion." These buttons were dried and the fuzz removed from the top before being ingested.

The effects from eating the buttons were twofold. First, the individual would experience the impact of a set of alkaloids that could produce symptoms similar to drinking several cups of strong coffee: a higher pulse rate and a flushed face. In time these would be replaced by the effects of other alkaloids that greatly heightened sensitivity to sound and color. This enabled the user to see brilliantly colored visions, hear the sun rise, or have the sensation of floating in air supported by the sound of the ceremonial drum. A common experience was to have the sense of being a detached observer outside one's body. With no grasp of how the alkaloids could affect body chemistry, it is not strange that Indians attributed to peyote a supernatural power. And it had other valuable functions. While still a warrior on the plains, Quanah was reported to have worn a button on his chest as an amulet to help ward off enemy blows. Other warriors used it when trailing the enemy because of its power to sharpen their eyesight and hearing.

As wide-ranging hunters and raiders, the Comanches could have learned of peyote in many ways. Omer C. Stewart theorizes that the most likely Indians to have acquainted the Comanches with it were the Lipan and Mescalero Apaches. Thus Quanah's marital connection with the Mescalero may account for his introduction to peyote, or he simply might have made its acquaintance through older Comanches. Regardless of how he came to know peyote, it is certain that Quanah was familiar with it by the time he reported in to Fort Sill in 1875. And it is reasonable to assume that he subsequently partook of it whenever it was available. Indeed, his trips to New Mexico may have been motivated in part by his desire to obtain buttons. We do know that in December 1884 Quanah stopped by Fort Davis in West Texas, on a mission to obtain "a certain herb which they prize as medicine," according to an officer in the local garrison.

The traumatic events of the mid-1870s, which forcefully ended for the Comanches a free and happy life on the plains and subjected them to a new and degraded existence, would have made them anxious for any psychological reinforcement. A plant that could at least temporarily give them the experience of escaping the terribly depressing reality of reservation life would have been eagerly welcomed. Moreover, finding power through peyote fitted in well with the individualistic approach of Comanches to religion. Unlike their neighbors the Kiowas, who stressed a tribal rite, the Sun Dance, Quanah's people left it to each man to be his own priest. Worshiping as individuals or in small groups also made peyote ceremonies less conspicuous.

Like slaves on a plantation, the Comanches quickly learned, and none better than Quanah, the necessity of telling the white man what he wanted to hear, while preserving as much of the old way of life as possible. Just as Quanah did not brag of his exploits as a raider, neither did he flaunt his use of peyote.

Only slowly did agency officials become cognizant of the Comanche chief's devotion to peyote. In 1883 E. L. Clark, a well-known squaw man and agency employee, reported the presence on the reservation of an Indian "with some of those poison roots which Quanah and Black Bear[d] used to be so crazy to get hold of." According to Clark, the Indian was holding meetings in which the participants would eat the peyote, "which acts directly upon their brain and throws them into sort of a dream, and after recovery they conclude that they have had a devine [sic] revelation."

Agent Lee Hall, under the heading "Gambling and Other Crimes" in his 1886 annual report, referred to the Comanches and a few Kiowas eating "the tops of a kind of cactus . . . and it produces the same effect as opium." Hall feared that the habit was spreading and was "evidently injurious." He suggested that peyote be declared contraband. The agent apparently was reacting to another report by E. L.

Clark in which he described it as available at several stores just off the reservation, which would indicate a market for peyote at least several years old. Clark also ascribed to the Quahadas the origins of reservation peyote use and told of the Indians of that band consuming twenty to fifty each in a meeting, certainly an exaggeration.

Hall's successors, E. E. White, William D. Myers, and Charles E. Adams, also voiced concern about peyote use. White took over the agency in late 1887 and within a few months had received an anonymous letter charging that three white men who had purchased buttons from a merchant in Texas were offering them for sale to Comanches in the camps of Eschiti and Quanah. By June 1888 the agent had become sufficiently alarmed at what he heard about peyote to ban it: "Being convinced from what I learn from various sources . . . that many Indians on this Reservation are using Mescal Beans [a local term for peyote] to the extent of impairing their minds and physical strength: that some Indians have died from the excessive use of these beans: that they are in fact destructive to both the health and mental faculties of these Indians, and will greatly decimate them, if their use is not checked."

The Indians were ordered not to eat the buttons or drink "any decoction or fermentation thereof." White threatened violators of his order with loss of annuity goods, rations, and the grass money from the leases. Transmitting a copy of his order to the Indian commissioner, the agent made clear why merchants near the reservation were dealing in peyote. He estimated that they were selling, for never less than a dollar a button, an item that cost them only a few cents.

The Comanches stalled when confronted with White's ultimatum. At first they said that peyote was one of two things they refused to surrender, the other being plural wives. However, after the agent had conferred with a group of Comanches at Fort Sill, lecturing them on the ill effects of peyote, they agreed at least to try to give it up—after they had consumed their present supply. White was pleased to inform the Indian commissioner, only a month after he had published the ban, that Quanah had come to the Anadarko agency office with a message from the chiefs and headmen that their followers "had almost entirely quit using the bean." That is what White wanted to hear, and that is what Quanah told him.

In his annual report rendered in August 1888, Agent White went into some detail in recounting his own fight against peyote, or "Woqui," as he said the Comanches called it. White included a description of the button: "In size it is about one-fourth of an inch thick and 1½ inches in diameter. When dry it is hard and about the color of bright tobacco, and it is not unlike tobacco in taste. The center of the upper side is covered with a coat of gray fuzz." White went on to charge that peyote "not only makes physical wrecks of them in a short time, but it destroys their mental faculties as well." And he said that the Indians under its influence were "in dreamland and see the most beautiful visions." The only specific evidence the agent offered of damage done to individuals involved a Comanche who shot at his wife three times. The Indian had suspected her of infidelity, and peyote he had eaten told him to shoot at his wife. If he killed her, she was guilty; if he missed her, she was innocent. She was proved innocent in the trial by gunfire; nevertheless the nonbeliever White had the husband arrested and dispatched to Texas for trial in a federal court.

Despite this episode, the agent expressed confidence that the Comanches would live up to their pledge to cease using peyote, as "they have the highest sense of honor and the most proper regard for their obligations of any Indians in the country." White was gone within a month of penning that optimistic prediction, and his replacement, William D. Myers, who lasted barely a year, saw no improvement. Agent Myers concluded that peyote use was "alarmingly on the increase" and would "finally make slaves and kill them with the same certainty that the morphine, opium, or alcohol habits kill the white man."

Myer's successor, Charles E. Adams, also waged an unsuccessful campaign against the devilish herb, ordering his Indian police to confiscate it and to arrest and deliver to the agency for punishment all users. This was not the type of order the police were likely to carry out with enthusiasm. Not only would it have brought them into conflict with some of the chiefs and headmen, but the police force itself included peyote devotees. The extant records of the Court of Indian Offense records reveal no cases involving use of the buttons.

There was ample evidence of the growing popularity of peyote on the agency's two reservations. And sometimes the sources could be pinpointed. A partner in a grocery business in Vernon, Texas, admitted to having on hand five or six thousand buttons, although he pled ignorance of its use being in violation of the law. The merchant was on sound ground there, as peyote had not been the subject of congressional legislation. Moreover, the dealer said his firm was not the only one handling peyote, although he did promise to cease and desist.

By May 1891 Agent Adams had despaired of ever curtailing its use as long as the merchants south of the Red River were permitted to sell it freely. "I reason with the Comanches and threaten," Adams confided in another agent, "but it does no good. They keep it hid out like the whites do whisky in Kansas." He was addressing his counterpart at the Ponca Agency, who had expressed his own concern

that some of the Tonkawas under his administration were obtaining
peyote from the Comanches. That Quanah's people, who had feared
and reviled the Tonkawas as trackers for troop columns, should share
with them peyote was indicative of its role in an expanding pan-
Indian movement.

By the early 1890s Comanches were practicing the peyote ceremony
in all its essentials. These, however, had variants, just as Christians
worship the same God but differ in their choices of hymns, vestments,
religious objects, and ceremonies. On the South Plains the rite that
Quanah had a major role in evolving and propogating was an all-
night ceremony, participated in only by males, and concluded by
breakfast shared by the communicants.

The ceremony took place in a tepee. On entering, the communicant
faced a raised altar that among Quanah's people took the form of a
horseshoe whose open end faced the tepee entrance. Atop the altar
would have been a single large peyote button, the "peyote chief" or
"father peyote," and in front of it a fire. The ceremony required a
minimum of a drum, a rattle, a staff, an eagle-bone whistle, a quantity
of sage, and a supply of buttons. As the participants entered, they
would move to their left and proceed to their sagebrush-filled cush-
ions behind and on the sides of the altar.

The actual worship was presided over by the "Road Man," a title
held by Quanah. This individual would have been tutored by another
Road Man and accepted as such by those who worshiped under his
ministry. This religious leader would begin the night's activities by
singing an opening song, holding the staff in his left hand while
shaking a rattle in his right to the accompaniment of the rhythms
provided by the "Drum Chief." A prayer smoke followed, and after
that there was the first ritual eating of peyote. Then, in succession
and moving counterclockwise, the participants each sang a series of
songs. At midnight the Road Man would interrupt proceedings to
offer a special song and then step from the tepee to face the four
cardinal directions and blow his eagle-bone whistle. At that point
drinking water would be brought to worshipers, then more songs
and ingesting of peyote followed until dawn, which the Road Man
heralded with a special chant. This was the signal for his wife, in the
role of the goddess Peyote Woman, to bring to the communicants
another bucket of water and bowls of sweetened corn, dried fruit,
and boneless meat.

The breakfast ended the formal peyote meeting, although the participants would remain together, discussing the significance of their
visions and the new songs introduced, before a leisurely noon meal
with friends and relatives. Apparently there was no hangover effect,
and the communicants emerged from the ceremony strengthened by

an internal peace and harmony and rededicated to loving their fellow man and strengthening their family ties.

During these years elements of Christianity were melded with the original native features. Quanah himself later defended the peyote-centered worship, declaring, "The white man goes into his church house and talks *about* Jesus, but the Indian goes into his tipi and talks *to* Jesus." The infusion of Christian elements into the Indian religion did not propitiate the missionaries, who during Quanah's lifetime were among its leading critics. J. J. Methvin, a Methodist minister who arrived on the reservation in 1887, recorded his recollections of a peyote meeting he happened into the following year. One night while visiting among the Comanches, he was attracted by the sound of drumming. Following the sound to its source, Methvin discovered a tepee where he concluded worship of some type was taking place. Two of Quanah's wives were lying on the grass near the tepee's entrance and, on being asked what was happening, gestured to him to enter. Raising the flap, he did so; while the worshipers, with eyes closed, continued their chants to the accompaniment of the drum and rattle, Methvin wound his way to a seat among them. When the song was completed, Quanah recognized the missionary and made him welcome.

The Comanche chief, as was customary, had come to the meeting carefully attired in native fashion. He wore a handsome fringed buckskin shirt, leggings, and moccasins. Quanah had applied face paint and plaited his hair, encasing it in strips of fine fur. For his unexpected guest he provided an explanation of the ceremony, observing that the Indians, in Methvin's words, "got their inspiration from the Great Father, while the white man got his through the book they have."

The missionary must have remained until dawn because he referred to the food being brought to the tepee by the women the following morning. Methvin also described the altar and father peyote as "a sort of horse shoe furnace with the open part extending toward the east, while on the summit of this little furnace was placed a large peyote button, toward which special deference was shown as they worshipped." Methvin was not favorably impressed, concluding that what he had observed was "purely a drug habit, and in recent years there has been projected into it the religious feature for protection in its use." He clearly had no grasp of the all-encompassing role of the supernatural in Comanche life. However, even modern scholars like La Barre have dismissed the Christian elements as "window-dressing for a proselytizing cult." The same could as easily be said of its competitor, the Ghost Dance Movement, which made its appearance on the South Plains in 1890 and also included Christian features.

Morning after a peyote ceremony, 1893. *Seated, second from left:* Quanah; *standing, at left:* two of his wives, Cho-ny and To-nar-cy. (*Courtesy National Anthropological Archives, Smithsonian Institution.*).

Indians responded to the teachings of Wovoka for some of the same reasons that they were attracted to the peyote ceremonies. Wovoka promised a renewal of the good life. Moreover, he assured the faithful that the white man would disappear and the game would return in numbers as great as those of the halcyon days of their grandfathers.

Like Christianity and the Peyote Cult, the Ghost Dance movement came in a variety of forms. There were differences, for example, about the circumstances under which the whites would disappear. The most common explanation was that a new layer of earth was moving from the northwest at glacial speed, astride it buffalo, wild horses, and all the other animal life. White men could either remain in place and be buried, or they could flee before it, finally to reembark for the lands of their forefathers. The version propagated on the South Plains, however, was less antiwhite. In whatever version, the Ghost Dance offered a vision that provided hope and solace for those reared as free-ranging plains dwellers but now stranded on reservations and subjected to constant pressure to give up fundamental beliefs and cherished life-styles.

By the summer of 1890 Comanches had heard that somewhere to the north Christ had returned to earth and that Indians were worshiping him with new ceremonies. Two Indians from the adjacent Cheyenne and Arapaho Reservation had traveled north in the spring and returned with information about making Ghost Dance shirts and the proper procedures for conducting the dance. Then Sitting Bull, a Southern Arapaho who had lived for many years with Northern Arapahoe relatives, returned to report that he had actually seen the Indian messiah Wovoka. Sitting Bull also was prepared to instruct ("give the feather to") other Indians he felt qualified to be leaders in the new faith. His procedure was to train seven men from each interested tribe, each of the disciples receiving a painted and consecrated eagle tail feather as a warrant of his new status. Kiowas were the first to receive the feather on the reservation they shared with the Comanches and the Kiowa-Apaches, and Sitting Bull also inducted neophytes from among tribesmen of the Wichita Reservation.

Both military and civilian officials were alarmed by the growth of the new development. Fort Sill's commandant ordered Lieutenant H. L. Scott, who commanded a new all-Indian cavalry troop, to keep the new religious movement under surveillance. Scott, who was genuinely interested in Indians and became an authority on sign language, followed the Ghost Dance activities closely in the winter of 1890–91. He concluded that it not only posed no threat but actually was beneficial. The officer dubbed Sitting Bull a "copper colored John the Baptist" and praised him for preaching honesty, monogamy, and brotherhood with all men, including the whites. Scott maintained that Sitting Bull "has given these people a better religion than they had before, taught them precepts which if faithfully carried out will bring them into better accord with their white neighbors and has prepared the way for their final Christianization, and for this he is entitled to no little credit." Finally, Scott raised the issue of religious freedom, arguing that to interfere with the dances would be "contravening the law," which gave to each individual the right "to worship God according to the dictates of his own conscience."

Lieutenant Scott reported also that the Comanches had sustained their reputation for religious skepticism by showing little interest in what Sitting Bull had to offer. He was joined in this by Major Wirt Davis, who had been ordered to the scene by authorities alarmed at the potential for bloodshed, a potential to be fulfilled horribly at the Wounded Knee Massacre of Big Foot's band of Miniconjou Sioux. But the Ghost Dance that Davis and Scott observed reminded the major of "an old fashioned Methodist or Baptist camp meeting," and the major had some flattering remarks to make on Quanah in his report.

Quanah's opposition to the new movement was clear from the start. In May 1890, when rumors about it were just reaching the South Plains, he went on record in a letter to the agent, using a secretary whose writing skills left something to be desired: "I hear the koway and Shianis Say that there are Indians come from heaven and want me to take My People and go to see them. But I tell them that I want my People to work and pay no attention to that that we Depend on the Government to help us and no them."

Six months later Quanah felt it necessary to correct a Fort Worth paper that had accused him of being a Ghost Dance leader and bent on stirring up the Indians. He vehemently denied attending any Ghost Dances or meeting with Sitting Bull. Quanah insisted that "but few of the Comanche Indians pay any attention to the Messiah craze, and those who do are crazy." He also questioned the sanity of any Indian who plotted an uprising, given "the little handful of warriors that all the tribes could combine and turn out." After referring to his farm and new house "that would be called a good house in any country," Quanah declared, "Having just got fixed to live comfortably, I would be worse than an idiot to incite my people to do something that would make beggars and vagabonds of them." The chief concluded, "We have been accused of most everything except being fools, and people who know the Comanches have never credited them with that."

Beyond the reasons he cited, Quanah might have mentioned others that must have played a role in setting the tone of his letter. It was during this time period that he had been seeking government support to complete his house, while at the same time Quanah's "much married condition" was being made the subject of critical examination by the Indian commissioner. This was no time for him to be identified with a phenomenon as disturbing to the white officials as the Ghost Dance. And Quanah, of course, was already deeply involved in peyotism. That cult had satisfied a spiritual need of the chief and many of his Comanche followers. Moreover, he could not have been pleased at the competition from the new faith identified with the Arapahoes and Kiowas on the South Plains. As an acknowledged leader and innovator in the practice and dissemination of peyote worship, Quanah was unlikely to turn to a religion in which Kiowas had taken the lead on the reservation they shared.

But whether Comanches or Kiowas, peyotists or Ghost Dancers, the Indians were facing a new and dangerous threat to what remained of their old way of life. This was the loss of most of the land they held in common and the allotment of the rest as individually held farms.

CHAPTER 6

A Tough
but Realistic Negotiator

IN December 1886 an inspector from Washington was on the reservation several days. In his report he proposed that the Comanches, as the most "pliable" of the Indians there, be introduced to the blessings of severalty—private property in land. Agent Hall also subscribed to this view and estimated, with no apparent basis in fact, that as many as 150 of the Comanches, Kiowas, and Kiowa-Apaches wished their own allotments. Hall asked that the Indian Office dispatch surveyors to begin the process, but nothing came of it.

Two decades earlier the framers of the Treaty of Medicine Lodge had made provision for the extension of severalty to these Indians. A clause in the 1867 treaty authorized heads of family to sequester for their own use up to 320 acres, with those over eighteen entitled to eighty acres. "At any time," the president might have the entire reservation surveyed and Congress could then "fix the character of the title" for each Indian's chosen plot.

There had been no rush by the Indians to avail themselves of this opportunity. Indeed, only the wife of a squaw man requested her 320 acres, and that manifestly was at the initiative of her white husband. Despite the proposals of the inspector and the agent in 1886, if anything could unite the reservation's badly divided population, it was their opposition to severalty.

The General Allotment Act of 1887, usually referred to as the Dawes Act, after its principal architect Senator H. L. Dawes, was Congress's contribution to making allotment in severalty applicable to tribes. It authorized the president, when he thought it desirable, to have reservations surveyed and individual farms allotted to the Indians. Any land remaining, the so-called surplus left after each head of family had received 160 acres of land, with smaller amounts to others, would then be purchased by the United States "for the sole purpose of securing homes to actual settlers." Reformers could support the

Dawes Act because they sincerely believed that private property was a civilizing agent, and settlers backed it because of the possibility of millions of acres becoming available for their exploitation. The law was hardly enacted before Agent Hall was reporting resistance to it from his charges. Lone Wolf, the Kiowa chief, was in Washington only a few days after the passage of the Dawes Act and personally expressed to the Indian commissioner his hostility to severalty for his people. The commissioner responded with a defense of private property as "the foundation of all permanent civilization and independence," although he assured Lone Wolf that under no circumstance would the reservation be among the first to be surveyed and allotted. Two months later at a council at Anadarko, Lone Wolf again inveighed against severalty and was supported by a few other speakers. They included White Wolf, who had been allied with the Tabananaka faction that had opposed Quanah in tribal politics.

While any reservation Indian might be alarmed at the prospect of severalty, that Lone Wolf had been so vocal was the result of his having met with Dr. Thomas A. Bland while in Washington. Dr. Bland was one of the founders of *Council Fire*, a periodical "devoted to the civilization and rights of the American Indian," according to its masthead. Although, like most of the white reformers of that day, he had originally supported severalty as essential to the civilization of the Indian, Bland had cooled on the idea. Another Kiowa reported that Bland had cautioned Lone Wolf against severalty, because it "is a detriment to your people, and I, as a friend of yours, advise you not to be too hasty in accepting allotments, because the moment you accept the proposition you are gone."

There is no evidence that Quanah ever met Dr. Bland; nevertheless, he also had good reason to oppose allotment in severalty. Wherever Indians held land in common, it had been the most acquisitive, frequently mixed-bloods, who had profited most from the tribe's resources, whether it be pasture, farm land, timber, or minerals. By the early 1890s Quanah had under his control a pasture that contained, by the highest estimate, 44,000 acres. He needed range for his several hundred head of cattle and horses, but that still left him in possession of thousands of acres that could be rented to ranchers wishing to run cattle on Indian land. And the proceeds from those transactions went into Quanah's pockets, not the Comanche treasury. He also was on the payroll of the Texas cattlemen who leased, at bargain prices, over a million acres of Comanche grass. These ranchers would be driven from the reservation if the severalty policy were implemented, to be replaced by thousands of non-Indian farm families. The Texans practically had Quanah on retainer to represent their interests, which definitely included opposing allotment in severalty. When this is coupled with his followers' united front against severalty and his understandable reluctance to being reduced to a relatively tiny 160-acre allotment, we can easily understand why Quanah tried for a decade to delay the imposition of severalty on the Comanches.

In March 1889 Congress took another step on the road that led to allotment for the Comanches. It created a three-man Cherokee Commission, later referred to as the Jerome Commission, after its chairman David H. Jerome. It was charged with negotiating with the tribes west of the ninety-sixth degree of longitude in the Indian Territory, in order to secure from them "the cession to the United States of all their title." By the time it had finished its work, the commission would have dealt with over twenty tribes and acquired from them fifteen million acres to be opened to non-Indian settlement. The tribes involved included the Cherokees, whose "Outlet" was occupied by cattlemen, the Cheyennes and Arapahos, and those tribes of the two reservations administered by the agent at Anadarko.

Within six months of the creation of the commission, Quanah was petitioning his agent to permit him to travel to Washington. He had heard a rumor from some Cherokees that Jerome and his colleagues soon would be visiting the Comanches, and he wished to speak to the Washington authorities first. At that time the Indian commissioner refused him permission to visit the capital, but Quanah persisted. There was some urgency in his appeals, as the pasture leases negotiated in 1884 were about to lapse, and the Texas cattlemen were anxious to have them renewed. A new agent, Charles E. Adams, now presided at Anadarko, and he endorsed Quanah as "a particularly progressive Indian" who should be permitted to proceed to Washington.

In June 1890 Quanah did reach the capital, at the expense of the cattlemen. As usual there was no united front among the Comanches on the issues facing them. Quanah was urging the employment of an attorney to represent them in their land disputes with the federal government, and White Wolf and other chiefs were opposing him. In a letter to the Indian commissioner, White Wolf denounced Quanah as a "white man" who "always want to do his own way." Agent Adams saw the conflict as primarily being between the Quahadas and the Yamparikas and spoke of the "constant friction" between the leaders of the Comanche divisions. While describing Quanah to the Indian commissioner as more progressive than most of his rivals, the agent maintained that Quanah had his faults and was in Adams's office, "at this moment dressed in buckskin with blanket."

After a lot of administrative backing and filling, the secretary of the interior finally authorized pasture lease negotiations. In February 1892 the Indians selected Quanah, Lone Wolf, and White Man, a Kiowa-Apache, to go to Washington to try to get the matter settled.

They were accompanied by their agent and also by an attorney for two of the Texas cattlemen applying for extension of their leases. In a campaign to defeat this, representatives of Texans interested in farms that could be carved from the reservation complained to the secretary of the interior of Quanah's being "regularly in the employ of Burnett and Waggoner." They also charged that the chiefs simply were trying to maintain their tribal authority, which would suffer if the reservation were open to settlement. On the recommendation of Quanah's delegation and the Indian commissioner, however, the secretary approved one-year leases for the Big Five—Burk Burnett, Dan Waggoner, C. T. Herring, E. C. Suggs, and J. P. Addington— for a total of nearly 1,250,000 acres at six cents per acre. Because of their good record as tenants, the Big Five were not required to engage in competitive bidding to secure their leases. That was a condition the Interior Department insisted upon for about 250,000 additional acres. Nevertheless, the income per acre from the competitive bidding was slightly less than the six cents received from the Big Five.

Quanah was home from Washington only briefly before departing again, this time on one of his junkets to the Mescalero Apache Reservation. When he returned, he busied himself with a porch-building project for his house. That was interrupted by the arrival at the agency of the three-man Cherokee Commission delegated to persuade the Comanches, Kiowas, and Kiowa-Apaches to accept allotment in severalty and to sell their surplus land to the United States. Quanah would play a major role in those negotiations.

The commissioners arrived at Fort Sill on September 19, 1892, and by October 22, after a dozen meetings, claimed success. The chairman, David H. Jerome, had been governor of Michigan and for five years was a member of the Board of Indian Commissioners. This latter experience had acquainted him with the problems Indians faced, although there was no sign that he had developed any sympathy for their plight. His own commission employed some of the tactics government officials had used since the founding of the republic to coerce Indians into ceding land, including threats as well as bribes for interpreters, Indian leaders, and influential local whites.

At the first public meeting of the commission with the tribesmen, at which the Comanches were better represented than the Kiowas or Kiowa-Apaches, since it was held at Fort Sill, Jerome made his opening pitch. He informed the Indians that they no longer needed a large reservation and that "now you have the opportunity to sell to the Great Father all the land that you cannot use for homes for his white children." The other two commissioners, Alfred M. Wilson of Indiana and Warren G. Sayre of Arkansas, also spoke. Sayre took the opportunity to remind the Indians of the Dawes Act, under whose

Quanah, ca. 1892. (*Courtesy Archives & Manuscripts Division of the Oklahoma Historical Society, no. 14202.*)

terms the president, "whenever he pleases," could "require" the Indians to take their allotments. "We do not know when such an order will be made, or that such an order will ever be made," Sayre warned; "we only say that the power resides in the Great Father to make the order any time." That threat would be resorted to again and again to coerce the Indians into accepting the terms the commission would dictate for the United States purchase of what was euphemistically referred to as their "surplus" land, that acreage remaining after each Indian had received his or her allotment.

After a few comments by Tabananaka, Quanah took the floor. He informed the commissioners that he had been expecting them and had cautioned his people against any hasty decision: "Do not go at this thing like you were riding a swift horse, but hold up a little." Quanah referred to his interview a few months earlier with Commissioner of Indian Affairs Thomas J. Morgan, and how Morgan had told him that Jerome and his colleagues could only promise certain sums for the Indians' land—"buy it with mouth-shoot" was Quanah's blunt way of putting it. "Now," he said, speaking like someone who had been wheeling and dealing with canny Texas ranchers for eight years, "I want to know how much will be paid for one acre, what the terms will be, and when it will be paid."

Jerome tried to cut off that line of discussion by responding that Quanah would get answers to his questions "by and by." The Comanche chief was not to be dismissed so lightly. He demanded to know, "When will you answer the questions?" Jerome again temporized, but Quanah would not shut up. He said that some of the Indians were interested only in the prospect of getting some cash in their hands, but "I want a thorough understanding. . . . I just want to talk about business, talk to the point." Jerome and his colleagues had been put on notice that at least one Comanche chief, despite his inability to speak more than a little English, had a good grasp of how one did business in the white man's world. Quanah had had an education at the hands of tough ranchers and businessmen like Burk Burnett and Dan Waggoner.

At the meeting the next day other Indians spoke first. They were Stumbling Bear and Big Tree of the Kiowas, and two Comanches: Howeah, who had signed the Treaty of Medicine Lodge a quarter century earlier, and Eschiti. The Kiowas made clear their reluctance to abide by allotment and to sell the surplus land; however Howeah indicated his willingness to accept the commission's proposal, even though the terms had yet to be revealed. Eschiti, remembered as the medicine man at the Adobe Walls fight and the chief who had led the Quahadas in to Fort Sill in June 1875, asked that allotment be delayed until the 1867 treaty's thirty-year provisions for annuities and other government assistance had lapsed. As did the Indians generally, except for Quanah, Eschiti stressed in his pronouncements his dependence on the Great Father and "a father located with us [the agent] to learn what to do." He also, however, acknowledged Quanah's role: "Quanah has things, as it were, written on his tongue. What he

Quanah and wives To-pay and Cho-ny, ca. 1892. (*Courtesy Western History Collections, University of Oklahoma Library.*)

learns from the Government he writes on his tongue, and we learn from him."

David Jerome responded to these Indians by trying to reassure them that it was not being proposed that they move. They and their children, Jerome declared, could occupy their allotments "for all time." He said each Indian would be able to select his or her own tract.

Quanah then raised the issue of how much land each Indian would get, reminding his audience that the provision in the Treaty of Medicine Lodge had been for 320 acres. And he added that he also wanted to know how much per acre the government proposed to pay for the surplus that remained after allotment of the Indians. The chairman tried to evade the issue, but Quanah persisted, "You have not told us how much land you propose for one Indian to have nor how much for one acre." That finally elicited the information that each Indian would receive a 160-acre allotment. Commissioner Sayre defended this on the grounds that while not as much as the 320 acres for heads of families provided for in the 1867 treaty, for a family with several children it actually would mean more land.

Sayre also eventually got around to making the government's offer for the surplus land: $2 million. But Quanah wanted to know how much that would be per acre, seeking some way of comparing it with what the United States had paid other tribes. That led to an interesting exchange as recorded in the council minutes:

Quanna Parker: How much per acre?
Mr. Sayre: I can not tell you.
Quanna Parker: How do you arrive at the number of million dollars if you do not know?
Mr. Sayre: We just guess at it.

Sayre did go on to explain that there were certain variables difficult to evaluate, such as estimating how many Indians there would be to take allotment by the time the agreement was finally ratified by Congress. Nor could the commissioners predict how successful the Chickasaws and Choctaws might be in claiming a share of any price paid, on the grounds that the reservation had been a part of their Leased District. This was an area that in 1855 the United States had obtained to house other tribes. The Chickasaws and Choctaws, on similar grounds, had managed to get a larger share of the price the United States had paid for the Cheyenne and Arapaho Reservation than the Cheyennes and Arapahoes themselves had received. Nevertheless, Quanah believed, and with good cause, that the commissioners were trying to deny the Indians information they needed to bargain effectively for the best price for their land.

Before the next meeting the three tribes conferred individually and each concluded, at least for the present, not to accept allotment and sale of their surplus lands. Quanah did not speak at this third meeting, and he may not even have been present, although Indians who did attend reiterated their opposition and echoed Quanah's insistence on the commissioners' leveling with them about the government's offer per acre. Chairman Jerome, after referring to how "Yesterday Mr. Parker pushed Judge Sayre hard to tell him how much . . . for one acre," did come up with a figure. Allowing for several variables, Jerome estimated that they were offering "a trifle over $1" per acre. That he exaggerated by a factor of about 25 percent is apparent from Jerome's later report, for the eyes of Indian Commissioner Morgan, that they had paid only approximately eighty cents per acre.

At this meeting White Wolf referred to "a friend of ours," John T. Hill, who "can do something for us." Hill's contribution is unclear, although there are some clues. When the Cherokee Commission negotiated with the Kickapoos for their land, Hill helped break down Kickapoo resistance to allotment and was rewarded with $5,000 from the tribe's funds, when it should have been the United States Treasury that paid the bill, as he certainly was not working in the tribe's interest. Now Hill would serve as "advisor" to the Comanches and Kiowas without arousing the ire of the commissioners, so it may be surmised that he again was in league with the white men. Additional evidence of this was Jerome's willingness to make available to him the services of one of the official interpreters. Last but not least, Hill was one of the several white men who received a 160-acre allotment by the terms of the agreement, again, as had been the case with the Kickapoo agreement, being paid from Indian assets for helping sell them down the river.

Hill's function at the negotiations at Fort Sill and Anadarko seems to have been to undercut tribal resistance to a cession. He helped convince them that with the aid of an attorney they would be able to improve on the $2 million offer. Quanah went along with this tactic, even taking credit for it in open council: "I sent for a lawyer." But when Henry Asp appeared, the attorney's proposed commission of 7 percent seemed too much of a sting to the Indians. They were coached in this regard by Lieutenant H. L. Scott, who commanded the Indian cavalry troop at Fort Sill and usually worked to safeguard their interests. Lieutenant Scott pointed out to the Indians that Asp would expect 7 percent even of the $2 million, the minimum figure they were guaranteed, a tidy legal fee of at least $140,000 for no service rendered.

Meanwhile, the negotiations ground on. At one point Quanah remarked in open council, "We think that we understand what the commission has said to us, but do not think that the commission has understood what we have said." Quanah clearly was trying to drag out the bargaining and asked for a two-month delay, charging that any deal at this time was "impossible." But the commissioners continued to wear down the Indians' resistance. Chairman Jerome estimated that if a three-year postponement of allotment and sale of the surplus land took place, the Indians would lose $225,000 in interest on the $2 million. To drive home the point, Jerome said that would be the equivalent of 225 boxes of silver dollars, a load to haul which would require eight wagons with six-mule teams.

One of the arguments the commissioners had offered for not paying more than $2 million for the surplus land was that much of it was mountainous and rocky. This was certainly true of the boulder-strewn Wichita Range that ran through the reservation, although Quanah found a way to counter that argument: "The commission speaks of the rocks and hills being worthless, but I have noticed that coal is burned in such localities and that iron, silver and gold are found in such places." At a subsequent meeting he returned to the subject: "The mountains are all supposed to be rocks and the rocks are supposed to be worthless, but the military use them to make houses with, and you say that the Government does not propose to pay anything for this worthless land—rocks. We could let it go, but suppose some fellow should find gold in it."

Of all the Indians who spoke during the negotiations, only Quanah pressed the commissioners in a way suggesting comprehension of the process. He was the one who continually insisted on knowing the exact terms the commissioners were offering, observing, "I want to hear all the parts and various points. I know that the law is a very particular thing." Nor did Quanah delude himself that the agreement would be to his advantage: "I do not expect myself to bring my condition in much better shape by this trade." After all, he would be giving up access to an impressive 44,000-acre spread, in return for a minuscule 160 acres.

But Quanah knew that he could at best only delay, not stop, the juggernaut. On October 11 the commissioners produced a copy of the agreement they had drafted and began to collect signatures, principally Comanche. Quanah was one of those who signed in the three days before the commissioners moved on to Anadarko to make their arguments to the bulk of the Kiowas and Kiowa-Apaches. By that time, as Lieutenant Scott much later was to recollect it, the commissioners had greased the way by a variety of inducements. Quanah, Tabananka, and Lone Wolf presumably had been promised money, as had Joshua Given, the educated Kiowa who had served as one of the three interpreters. There is reason to doubt this version, but the draft of the agreement did make special provisions for other individuals who might expedite the Indians' acceptance.

Of the two other interpreters, one was included with eighteen whites to "be entitled to all the benefits of land and money conferred by this agreement." The lucky eighteen included several intermarried white men and the wife of Joshua Given. An additional seven "friends of said Indians who have rendered to said Indians valuable services" each would receive a 160-acre allotment. Besides the third interpreter, they were the slippery John T. Hill, Quanah's tenant David Grantham, Methodist missionary J. J. Methvin, the infant daughter of former Agent Charles E. Adams, current Agent George D. Day, and, none other than Lieutenant H. L. Scott. The possibilities for conflict of interest seemed limitless, yet none of these individuals asked that his or her name be withdrawn. During the ratification process, Congress proved hardly more sensitive but did drop the names of Day and Scott.

The draft was discussed with the Kiowas and Kiowa-Apaches in three sessions, the last one on October 17 being disrupted. After a heated exchange most of the Kiowas stormed out of the meeting. The commissioners, however, insisted on continuing a rump session. In the course of it Commissioner Sayre invoked Quanah: "When we first met it was a new thing, and a good many sensible headmen—Quanah had to understand it, and when he understood it he said it was good."

Quanah's exact role in bringing about the Jerome Agreement will never be known. He is the one Indian leader who might have temporarily blocked it. Alone among the three tribes he had a sufficient following and a grasp of what was going on. As his contributions in the early sessions demonstrated, Quanah asked the right questions and insisted on getting answers. Nevertheless, he also was shrewd enough to recognize that fighting a delaying action and trying to get the government's offer sweetened somewhat was the most that the Indians could hope to accomplish. As a result of his many trips to Washington, Quanah knew better than any other Indian on the reservation the government's intent to reduce tribal landholdings— and the futility of blind resistance. That he might have been offered, and accepted, the promise of special treatment is certainly within the range of possibility. Bribing Indian leaders was a time-honored tactic of the United States, and Quanah had been exposed for over fifteen years to a white culture that condoned cutting corners to achieve financial success. His role models had been Texas ranchers, agency officials, squaw men, traders, army officers, and even ministers, who on occasion did not flinch at unethical conduct in their drive for material gain. Senator Dawes had said that greed was the element most conspicuously lacking in Indian societies and that without it they could not hope to reach the white man's level of civilization. The senator would have been pleased to see that Quanah had progressed so far.

It would be eight years before Congress ratified the Jerome Agreement. In terms of relative prosperity, that period would be the best the Comanches would enjoy since their life on the plains had ended.

CHAPTER 7

High Tide for Quanah

FOR Quanah the years between the negotiation of the Jerome Agreement in 1892 and its ratification in 1900 proved to be the most affluent period of his reservation life. They also saw him confirmed in his position as *the* Comanche chief, after years of wrangling with fellow tribal members. While in these respects the best of times, it could be viewed as well as the worst of times, as the Indians were harassed by thousands of whites jockeying for position to be ready for the moment when two million acres of land would be thrown open to white settlement. In the newspapers of towns neighboring the reservation, "boomers" were extolling the land in terms better fitted to the Garden of Eden ("Beautiful to the eye, magnificent in resources, unsurpassed in the fertility of its soil"). Meanwhile, "sooners" were infiltrating the reservation by the thousands in the guise of tenants for Indian farms, prospectors for minerals in the Wichita Mountains, and travelers on the public roads crossing Indian land.

In the aftermath of the Jerome Agreement negotiation, Quanah and his fellow Comanches were intent on delaying its implementation as long as possible. Members of the Jerome Commission had assured them that it would take two or three years for the Congress to ratify the agreement, and the government would then need additional time to allot the Indians their 160 acres and arrange for the opening of the surplus lands to white settlers.

Quanah had his own reasons for trying to delay the opening as long as possible. One of them was the thousands of acres that had come to be known as the "Quanah pasture," on which he ran his own several hundred head of stock as well as cattle whose owners paid the Comanche chief for the privilege. His annual income for these two activities must have approximated $1,000. In addition he shared with other Comanches the grass money, rations, and annuities and had his own income from the cattlemen. Quanah could afford the good life by reservation standards.

It was in the cattlemen's cause that Quanah traveled to Washington in November 1892, only a month after his dealings with the members of the Jerome Commission. One of his principal concerns on this visit, as on several others before 1900, was the grazing leases, which were bringing the three tribes about $100,000 a year in 1892, a figure that would nearly double by 1900. Quanah's first order of business was to push for the renewal of the leases of the Big Five to over a million acres, as those contracts were due to expire April 1, 1893. There were a half dozen smaller leases that would lapse in August, but clearly Quanah was most concerned with those of the Big Five. Inasmuch as at a minimum they had provided him the railroad tickets for himself and wife To-nar-cy, his priority is understandable. He also submitted to the government a claim for reimbursement for his hotel bill, although this was disallowed. The cattlemen surely also had covered this expense, but Quanah was never reluctant to try to tap a likely source. After ten years of wheeling and dealing with the cattlemen, Quanah had developed the streak of acquisitiveness that whites deplored seeing so rarely in Indians.

While in Washington, he also broached the subject of several Comanche warriors who, rather than surrender at Fort Sill after the Red River War, had taken up residence among the Mescalero Apaches. They now had families on that reservation, and Quanah wished to arrange the transfer of these people to Oklahoma, over Mescalero objections to the removal of the wives and children. Quanah was in Washington in March 1894 and again raised the issue. This time the commissioner of Indian affairs authorized him to visit the reservation and make the arrangements—if the Mescalero leadership approved. Somehow Quanah pulled it off. Despite an angry Apache reaction at losing some of their people, a reaction that bordered on violence, he was able to bring back seven men, together with some of their wives and children. On hearing the details from the Mescalero agent, the Indian commissioner ordered Quanah to stop visiting that reservation. Nevertheless, the chief enjoyed his triumph, sharing it with a newspaperman from Marlow, a town adjoining the reservation on the east. Quanah truly savored the role of leader and protector of his people.

As a chief who owed his position to the agent, however, Quanah was expected to walk the white man's road, and that included persuading his followers to enroll their children in school and to set an example by sending his own. He was slow to do this, reflecting the general Comanche opposition to having their children educated at white schools. It was bad enough to send them, to the Fort Sill boarding school that opened in 1893, where boys would have their braids lopped off and both they and the girls forced to don uncomfortable shoes and school uniforms. Worst of all, even though the children would be no more than twenty miles from home, they were restricted to the institution, and their parents were not supposed to visit them more than once a month.

School and agency officials expressed pained surprise at the strong parental love that made Indian fathers and mothers so reluctant to part with their children. Resistance of mothers and fathers to sending their children to the school at Chilocco near the Kansas border, or to Carlisle in far-away Pennsylvania, was naturally even greater. The children were permitted to return home from Chilocco at the end of the school year, but Carlisle's founder Richard H. Pratt insisted in the 1890s that parents surrender their children to him for an entire five-year term. An alarming number of them—eleven of the first sixty to attend from the Anadarko agency–died at Carlisle or after returning home ill. It is no wonder that families who, under any circumstances, had difficulty seeing the virtues of a white man's education, had to be coerced into sending their children to boarding schools. To fill the quotas, agents denied rations to recalcitrant parents and even, in unusual cases, seized children and shipped them off to Chilocco without parental consent. As late as 1900, however, there still were not enough classrooms on the reservation for hundreds of the children, despite the government's pledge at Medicine Lodge in 1867 to provide education.

Although not until the 1890s did any of his many children attend, in time Quanah became a supporter of the government's education program. The only government boarding school on the reservation until 1893 was the one at Anadarko in the northern part of the reservation. The Comanches were reluctant to send their children that far away, particularly if they had to be enrolled with Kiowas, whom the Comanche parents maintained were a bad moral influence on their offspring. When the predominantly Comanche boarding school opened at Fort Sill, that excuse for keeping their children at home was lost. Three of the Parkers—Esther, Baldwin, and Laura— were enrolled at the Fort Sill school for varying periods. Esther, Wanada, and Baldwin also attended Chilocco, and Esther, Wanada, Laura, and Harold were students at Carlisle. Captain Pratt was particularly interested in attracting the children of influential chiefs, and he courted Quanah, inviting him to Carlisle for commencement and appointing him to the board of visitors for the school.

With the honor, however, went onerous responsibilities. On one occasion a visiting official from Washington, who was assisting Captain Pratt recruit students for Carlisle, directed the Comanches to provide nineteen. The official made Quanah responsible for finding seven, and assigned six other chiefs a quota of two each. As the agent's right-hand man among the Comanches, Quanah also could be expected to recruit for the Fort Sill school. In 1899 the agent informed him that "the children are not being gotten into school as fast as I wish and I want you to see that the school at Fort Sill is filled . . . so that I can write of that to the Commissioner in Washington."

Quanah's status meant that his children were more visible than those of less prominent Comanches and that at least some of them would have to be in school if Quanah was to pressure other parents to send theirs. Not that his children would necessarily become role models. One of his sons, Baldwin, who attended the Fort Sill school, was singled out by the superintendent of that institution as "the most worthless scamp in that tribe." That was after he had already run away from Chilocco.

His daughter Wanada remembered Quanah as a typical Comanche father—loving and indulgent. When she and a sister were at the Fort Sill school, her father brought them a porcelain pitcher and basin for their private use for fear of their catching trachoma from the other children. Learning on another occasion that she was ill at school, Quanah brought her beefsteak to supplement the school's meals. Never a strong child, Wanada suffered from arthritis, and she recalled her father treating her condition by massaging her leg and bathing it in hot, herbal remedies.

Neither Wanada nor any of her many siblings attended any of the five mission schools, which by 1900 provided alternatives to the government schools on the reservation. One of them operated by the Presbyterians and located on Cache Creek attracted a few Comanche children, but none of them Quanah's. To some of the Indians the missionaries seemed to display an unholy interest in land. It was customary for mission schools to be permitted to fence 160 acres or more for crops and pasture, and, as noted above, Reverend J. J. Methvin had been written into the Jerome Agreement for 160 acres for himself. Nevertheless, when Catholics and Mennonites sought permission to establish new missions in Quanah's area, Quanah was persuaded to lend his support.

The Catholics made their move in late 1889. Two priests first chose a location at the foot of Mount Scott, near Fort Sill, but Kiowas in the vicinity raised objections. These Indians also opposed the Catholics' selecting acreage nearer Fort Sill, although Kiowa-Apaches and Comanches consulted agreed to it—if Quanah approved. The two priests had a long conversation with the chief, and he gave the project his endorsement. It resulted in 1892 in the opening of Saint Patrick's Mission.

Five of Quanah's children, 1892. *Front:* Len and Baldwin; *back:* Wanada, Werahre, and Harold. (*Courtesy National Anthropological Archives, Smithsonian Institution.*)

Two years later it was the Mennonites who needed Quanah's cooperation. Reverend Henry Kohfeld was responsible for locating the mission, and he sought advice from Methodists and Baptists already in the field. Kohfeld learned from them that Quanah's support was necessary, and he sought him out. Quanah was absent when the minister and an interpreter called at his home, but To-pay, one of the chief's wives, responded sympathetically. Quanah returned home to hear her plea that he consent to the mission. The chief first discussed the matter with other Comanches and then mounted Kohfeld behind an Indian and led a party off to find a site. Stopping by a large post oak, Quanah dismounted and cut notches in the tree, telling the minister, "Here build Jesus House." Post Oak Mission was the result. A Mennonite missionary expressed his gratitude that "the Lord had honored his promise to His servant and answered the prayers of the committee and the Conference." There was room in Quanah's theology too for divine intervention, whether or not he actually had been the agent of the Lord in this instance.

While agents and some missionaries sang his praises, Quanah received decidedly mixed reviews from his fellow Indians in the nearly eight years that elapsed before the ratification of the Jerome Agreement. The differences arose over the issues of leasing, purchasing cattle with the grass money instead of distributing it per capita, hiring attorneys to represent the tribes, and the inevitable rivalries for positions of leadership. Opposition to allotment and opening the reservation was something on which the Indians were virtually unanimous, although even here there were differences over tactics and how long it was practical to resist. Quanah continued to be the representative of the ranchers seeking leases of reservation land. Between the drafting of the Jerome Agreement in the fall of 1892 and its final ratification in the spring of 1900, he visited Washington eight times, usually subsidized by the cattlemen. Although the charge that he was in the pay of the Texans was frequently made, supporting documentation is scarce. Only for a trip in 1898 do the agency files yield copies of letters Quanah sent requesting funding. From Burk Burnett he asked $100, and Dan Waggoner was tapped for $300. These were two of the Texans with whom Quanah had the closest and most enduring business relationship.

As the leases generally were renegotiated in April, the pattern was for Quanah to go to Washington early in the year, with or without official approval. He usually was accompanied by an interpreter, two or three other Indian leaders, and sometimes To-nar-cy. A few times while he was in the East, Quanah was able to go to Carlisle to see his children enrolled there. On one occasion, Captain Pratt permitted

Quanah and To-nar-cy in Washington, 1895. (*Courtesy National Anthropological Archives, Smithsonian Institution.*)

Laura and Esther the rare privilege of taking the train to Washington to be with their father.

Early in 1896 two delegations from the reservation made their way east, stopping first at Carlisle and then going on to Washington. Quanah was accompanied by To-nar-cy, Eschiti, and Red Elk. Agent Frank D. Baldwin, an army captain detailed to the duty at Anadarko, had asked Quanah to see the Indian commissioner to discuss resurvey-ing the pastures to make certain that the Indians were being compen-sated for all the land being leased. Baldwin also authorized another delegation consisting of two Kiowas, Lone Wolf and Chaddle-kaungky, to visit Carlisle and Washington.

At their stop in Carlisle the delegations were the featured attraction at an evening convocation. Both Quanah and Lone Wolf spoke briefly, the Kiowa through an interpreter, but the Comanche commu-nicated using his uncertain grasp of English: "I do not talk English very much. I been here four days. I look all at you. I find everything good. I come 2,000 miles west. Oklahoma, that's where I come from. Telegraph to commissioner, me want to see my children. I go down Washington. I tell what I see here. Government wants to open the Indian country. Indian he no ready yet, maybe half of it, they ready. That's what I come for. That's what I tell commissioner."

The reporter for this occasion was equally impressed by To-nar-cy's appearance, remarking on her "basque and skirt of gay colored material" and her high-heeled shoes. "Mrs. Parker's" diamond rings and gold watch also were noted, as was her neatly combed hair, which hung in a single braid tied with a red ribbon. Unlike her husband, To-nar-cy spoke only Comanche.

When the delegation arrived in Washington, all five chiefs were present at a conference with the Indian commissioner. As usual, Quanah dominated the Indian side of the dialogue. He declared that three tribes opposed the opening of their reservation: "Some of us have good farms and houses but half are just Indian people, poor people who are not ready to be citizens." The commissioner offered them some reassurance on that point: "I cannot tell what Congress will do but we are trying very hard not to have it done and I hope it will not be."

Quanah also brought up other issues, including resurvey of the pastures and the construction of another school, the cost of which the agent had proposed should be shared jointly by the government and the tribes. Quanah emphasized the need for quick action on the new survey, as the leases were up for renewal April 1. The chief indicated that the Indians liked the idea of a new school, although they resented being asked to contribute almost half the cost of its construction: "We are too poor."

Eschiti and Red Elk, who were making their first visits to Washing-ton, had very little to say, as did Chaddlekaungky. The Kiowa, a judge on the reservation's Court of Indian Offenses, was apologetic: "You see we are large men but when you come to think of our minds we are like young calves who when they are first born do not know how to stand alone." Nevertheless, Chaddlekaungky was a major player in factional struggles that kept the reservation in turmoil during the late 1890s.

Quanah was right in the middle of the action as the ally of Agent Baldwin, who served from late 1894 to May 1898, when he was recalled for duty in the Spanish-American War. The chief likewise supported Baldwin's successor, William T. Walker, who held office barely a year. Both officials thought highly of Quanah, Baldwin giving him much of the credit for the Comanches' being, in the agent's opinion, "the most progressive and industrious" of the three tribes on the reservation. "He is solicitous for his people at all times," observed Baldwin, "and has accepted the inevitable change that must come to them."

But that was not the picture of Quanah that emerges from the statements of the other faction. It consisted of the principal traders on the reservation, some of the squaw men, the attorney who represented the three tribes from 1893 to 1898, a special agent from the Indian Office, and several prominent Comanches and Kiowas. Included at various times were Eschiti and Big Looking Glass of the Comanches, and Chaddlekaungky and Lone Wolf of the Kiowas.

Agent Baldwin, a strong-willed individual who had the distinction of being one of only two regular officers to win the Congressional Medal of Honor on two occasions, precipitated some of the bickering by policies that he initiated. He persuaded the Indians to divert $25,000 of grass money from the local traders' pockets to the purchase of cattle to be given each family. The traders could not attack this directly, so they brought charges that the contract under which the cattle were bought was tainted with fraud, Baldwin himself profiting illegally. The agent also undertook to do something about a few squaw men and Indian leaders monopolizing large pastures that they rented to others, siphoning off grass money that otherwise went into the pot to be divided among all the Indians. With just these two innovations Baldwin put himself at odds with powerful forces on the reservation—traders, squaw men, and some Indian leaders.

Attorney William C. Shelley, whom the three tribes had employed to represent them, was allied with the traders and intermarried white men. Shelley had resigned a position in the Indian Office to become the Indians' attorney. Although the tribesmen were concerned principally with getting someone to help them delay ratification of the Jerome Agreement, Shelley stressed their need of an attorney to defend them against depredations claims that totaled over $9 million. Frontier settlers who had lost property to raiding Indians could file claims for restitution. A frequent target for those claims were the "Fort Sill Indians," a generic term for raiding parties in the early 1870s when they could include warriors from several tribes and their terrified victims rarely were able to identify the Indians. Shelley could

Agent Frank D. Baldwin and tribal leaders, ca. 1895. *Seated:* Baldwin, Quanah, Apiatan, Apache John, and Big Looking Glass. (*Courtesy Museum of the Great Plains.*)

be effective in defending the Indians against such claims; he knew
his way around Washington and retained excellent contacts in the
Indian Office. Unfortunately, he felt it necessary to seek additional
clients among the squaw men and traders, thus creating potentially
serious conflicts of interest, as when traders opposed using tribal
funds to buy cattle.

Agent Baldwin's plan to use grass money to buy the cattle for
the Indians was based on his conviction—shared by most others
acquainted with the area—that stock raising, not farming, was the
only hope of the Indians' becoming self-supporting. Droughts were
simply too frequent for the tribesmen to depend upon raising crops.
Quanah, who already had a herd of cattle, supported the agent's plan.
And the Comanche chief was willing to go along with restrictions
on the access of squaw men to pastures, another Baldwin innovation.
The agent had uncovered one case in which a white man had been
renting a pasture for $300 a year, while subleasing it for $2,600. This
was a tidy profit for being the husband of a Comanche woman and
was only one of several ways squaw men took advantage of their
situation.

Agent Baldwin also was not reluctant to bring pressure on Indian
leaders to aid his reforms. When Quanah wrote Baldwin to tell him
that he was trying to limit the number of people spending time away
from their crops and livestock while drawing rations, he at the same
time proposed to bring five or six of his headmen to confer with the
agent. The agent's response was to direct that only one or two of the
headmen accompany their chief: "At this time of the year all the
people should be working in their fields and if the chief and head
men are running about the country it will be a bad example." When
the Indian chief of police reported an unusual amount of gambling
and peyote use among the Comanches, Baldwin called Quanah to
account: "I look to you for strong active support in breaking up these
customs which are so detrimental to your people, and must insist on
your close attention to accomplish this end. Please let me hear from
you in regard to this matter at your earliest convenience." Quanah's
response is not to be found, but Baldwin's reaction to it was to be
"very much relieved to receive the assurance that this report was very
much exaggerated." He concluded, however, with the injunction: "I
appreciate your efforts in trying to stop this injurious custom [pey-
ote], but you must not give up until you have succeeded perfectly."

The Comanche chief more than repaid Baldwin's giving him some
room on the peyote issue by loyally supporting the agent's projects
in councils on the reservation and in Washington, and in leading the
fight to fire attorney Shelley. Early in December 1897 thirty dissident
Indians had conferred and proceeded to select Eschiti as chief of the

Hugh L. Scott and tribal leaders, 1897. *First row:* Quanah, Scott, Big Looking Glass, and Apiatan. (*Courtesy National Anthropological Archives, Smithsonian Institution.*)

Comanches, and Frank Moetah to replace Quanah on the Court of Indian Offenses. Quanah reported this to Baldwin and explained it as a conspiracy involving attorney Shelley and Commissioner of Indian Affairs William A. Jones, who had just visited the reservation. The Comanche proposed that the agent retaliate by discharging, from a new reservation business committee, three of the Indians who had participated in the gathering of the dissidents. Quanah had a good grasp of the political principle of rewarding one's friends and punishing one's enemies.

But with Indian Commissioner Jones involving himself personally in reservation matters, Quanah and Baldwin faced serious opposition. Henry Wallace, a Mexican captive who was emerging as a leader of the anti-Baldwin Comanche faction, gave Commissioner Jones an account of the council that elevated Eschiti and deposed Quanah. As Wallace phrased it, Baldwin and Quanah "wand [sic] Mr. Shelley cut off we don't want that."

Another partisan who weighed in at this time was an official who would give both the agent and Quanah trouble—Gilbert B. Pray. Special Agent Pray, like other men in that position, served the Indian commissioner much as inspectors served the secretary of the interior. Special agents were troubleshooters, likely to turn up anywhere with orders to relieve an agent or conduct an investigation. What made it bad for Quanah and Baldwin was that Pray and William Shelley were close professionally, and both, despite the obvious impropriety, had invested in a mining company hopeful of striking it rich in the reservation's Wichita Mountains. Pray also had unusually close ties to his boss, Commissioner Jones, and spoke of "your friends and mine" in discussing traders and Shelley with the commissioner.

Baldwin credited Shelley with having enough clout with Commissioner Jones to get Quanah and Apiatan discharged from the Court of Indian Offenses early in 1898. The agent, in vain, defended Quanah and Apiatan and denounced their successors whom the commissioner himself had named—Chaddlekaungky and Frank Moetah. Meanwhile, about a hundred Comanches headed by Henry Wallace, Big Looking Glass, and Eschiti forwarded a petition to the Indian Office calling for the ouster of Chief Quanah: "He has worked against our welfare and interest and we have lost our confidence in him."

During the nearly four months before the outbreak of war with Spain led to Baldwin's being ordered to new duty, the struggle between the factions intensified. Each side had met in council and issued proclamations attacking their opponents, and each made full use of the mails to get their positions before the authorities in Washington. They also sent delegations to the capital.

Quanah's opponents demonstrated the range of their influence

Delegation to Washington, 1897. *Standing, at left:* Quanah; *seated:* To-nar-
cy, Apiatan, Apache John, and Big Looking Glass. (*Courtesy National Anthropological Archives, Smithsonian Institution.*)

when someone, probably attorney Shelley, arranged in late January
an invitation to seven of them to appear before the Senate Committee
on Indian Affairs. Included were Big Looking Glass, Eschiti, and
Henry Wallace. On learning of this, Quanah, and five of his allies
fired off a telegram protesting that those invited were not authorized
to represent the Comanches. A hastily called council nominated
Quanah, Apiatan of the Kiowas, and Apache John of the Kiowa-
Apaches, the tribal leaders Baldwin chose to recognize, to head another delegation to Washington.
    It would be a month before Quanah's delegation would leave for
the East; in the interim another big meeting would be held on the

reservation. At it, Quanah dismissed the Indians in Washington as handpicked by one of the traders and Shelley. The Comanche reminded the council that Shelley's contract expired in a few days and then prompted a resolution to hire a new attorney, one Charles P. Lincoln of Washington. The council appointed Quanah, Apiatan, and Apache John as a committee to work out the arrangements with Lincoln.

Not until mid-March did Quanah's delegation meet with the Indian commissioner in the capital, and when they did, the exchanges were, to use euphemisms of the language of diplomacy, frank and forthright. Quanah strongly defended himself by citing commendations he had received from Indian Commissioners Daniel M. Browning and Thomas J. Morgan, as well as Secretary of the Interior John W. Noble. Quanah also told of how he had responded to Commissioner Browning's criticism of his much-married state by inviting Browning to select which wife he should retain, a responsibility the commissioner declined to assume. And the chief responded to the charge that "I steal a great deal of money." He explained that when the cattlemen first came on the reservation, Indians killed and stole their cattle and that the white men had paid him to stop the depredations: "The money I got was from the cow men and not out of the lease fund." Commissioner Jones observed in rebuttal that one reason that the cattlemen offered for not being able to pay more than six cents per acre was that Quanah's services were so expensive. The Comanche chief was happier with Apache John's comment: "Those people who came here a short time ago may have told you that Quanah is a bad man; but I know better; he is just like light, you strike a match in a dark room and there is light; that is the way with Quanah, wherever he is is light. . . . The Indians think, some of them, because he is rich that he is better than they are and looked up to, and so they are jealous." Apache John failed to sway Indian Commissioner Jones, who remained supportive of the anti-Baldwin, anti-Quanah combination.

The wrangling on the reservation over hiring an attorney went on for months. At a council on April 9, of 220 male adult Indians present, 204 voted to fire Shelley, and 16 abstained. Reporting to Commissioner Jones, Gilbert Pray maintained that only a minority of the qualified voters had been present and declared that, "I cannot yield to the [Apiatan] and Quanah Parker element." He went on to claim the support of "all the old leaders of this people," listing, among others, Eschiti of the Comanches, and Big Tree and Chaddlekaungky of the Kiowas. Pray referred to his opposition as "the old crowd of Baldwin adherents," but the army officer had now been replaced by an Oklahoma journalist, William T. Walker.

Quanah and wives Mah-cheet-to-wooky, Cho-ny, and A-er-wuth-takum, ca. 1897. (*Courtesy National Anthropological Archives, Smithsonian Institution.*)

Shelley suffered the final defeat when another council was held June 17. Although the attorney and his ally Pray both addressed the Indians, the tribesmen literally lined up 360 to 269 against renewing Shelley's contract. They then authorized the hiring of Charles Lincoln, selecting Quanah, Apiatan, and Apache John to negotiate the contract. Quanah had won again.

But Quanah also suffered defeats in the marathon wrangling. He lost his seat on the Court of Indian Offenses, as discussed earlier, and the hike in the pasture rent from six cents to ten cents per acre was a blow to the Comanche chief and his Texas rancher employers. Burk Burnett had maintained in a letter to the secretary of the interior that it was impossible for ranchers to pay ten cents per acre and remain in business; nevertheless, he and others would manage.

Quanah was dealt an even more damaging blow by Special Agent Pray's effort to reduce the Comanche's rent free pasture holdings from an estimated 23,000 acres to 5,000, the new limit for all Indians and squaw men. Pray's pleasure in making the cut is apparent in a letter to Commissioner Jones: "I think the effect of this . . . on these Indians and on Parker the best thing I have done since I came here. . . . It brings Quanah to a level with other people and makes him divide with the people the big estate over which he has held kingly sway."

Pray's glee was shortlived, as Quanah continued to prove a difficult target. The chief would appear to be on the verge of signing a lease on Pray's terms, and then he would fail to follow through. The special agent began to suspect that Agent Walker was in Quanah's corner, just the latest of a long series of agents with whom the Comanche had made common cause. Nearly two months passed before Quanah signed a lease, and then he got a better deal than Pray had originally intended. Quanah retained control of the 23,000 acres, and after being allowed the 5,000 acres that was each Indian's right under the new dispensation and getting 10,000 acres exempted because it was barren mountains and hills, he had to pay the new ten-cent rate on 8,000 acres only. While this meant a substantial cut in Quanah's income, it was not the knockout blow Gilbert Pray had intended. Like other white men before him, the special agent had learned that Quanah was a shrewd businessman and canny politician.

Meanwhile Quanah was defending himself on other fronts. Special Agent Pray was complaining that Quanah and Apiatan "are determined to resist all efforts toward reconciliation" and were refusing to cooperate in the "breaking up of ghost dancing and mescal eating." Pray reported to Commissioner Jones that while Chaddlekaungky and Lone Wolf were informing on the ghost dancers and peyote users, that Quanah "went so far as to go into the convention of the missionaries and defend that conduct openly in an hour's speech." Three days later Pray was still complaining. Quanah and Apiatan "are defiant, and unrestrained," he wrote; "they are the recognized chiefs at this agency: they are consulted in everything and apparently protected in everything they do."

Methvin, the Methodist missionary, joined in the attack on Quanah and Apiatan. He denounced them as "the rankest polygamists" and

Quanah in his bedroom, ca. 1897. (*Courtesy Archives & Manuscript Division of the Oklahoma Historical Society, no. 705.*)

leaders in the peyote and Ghost Dance movements. Finally, Methvin charged that not only were the two chiefs keeping students from his mission school, but they were permitting them to enroll in a Catholic school, whose priest "declares himself favorable to the Ghost Dance and mescal eating."

By then Quanah was facing additional opposition in the form of a Quaker, Cyrus Beede, an inspector operating out of the office of the secretary of the interior. Formerly on the staff of the central superintendent during the hectic days when that official was trying to persuade the Comanches to take up residence on their reservation, Beede was persuaded to see the situation in 1898 from the viewpoint of Special Agent Pray. The inspector came up with a plan to counter what were now being referred to as "nonprogressive chiefs" such as Quanah and Apiatan. Beede proposed that they be replaced by a council of about a dozen Indians chosen to represent all three tribes. Special Agent Pray joined Inspector Beede in his proposal for what would be termed "a business committee." Pray quoted Lone Wolf as urging the creation of the committee "without a bigamist or mescal eater upon it." Quanah's opponents appeared to be winning the battle of the images. The advantage of being considered progressives was, at least temporarily, shifting to the faction headed by Eschiti and Lone Wolf.

Quanah, nevertheless, continued to enjoy a celebrity status rare for an Indian in western Oklahoma. Geronimo, an Apache confined to the reservation after having been moved there from Alabama in 1894, had a degree of notoriety, but Quanah was the Indian whose national recognition, hospitality, and comfortable residence attracted more visitors than he could afford to entertain. Typical was the small party of white men, one of whom was acquainted with Quanah, who timed a trip from Fort Sill so as to arrive at the chief's home at noon. They were served a meal, "such a one as one would expect at the home of a well-to-do farmer." The visitors spent the afternoon hiking in the mountains near the house, returning for dinner with Quanah and the four wives then in residence. The women did not speak English but otherwise deported themselves "much as well mannered white women." Although Quanah, as usual, declined to reminisce about his "deeds upon the war path," he did regale them with stories of his encounters with Washington officials and referred to some of the controversies on the reservation and his break with his old friend Eschiti. Quanah even told of taking a visiting inspector to a peyote meeting at which the white man ate several buttons and enjoyed himself thoroughly. Quanah explained this as the result of the peyote user envisioning that which most attracted him, whether it was piles of gold or "the happy hunting grounds."

At about the time that these white men descended on Quanah, he was plotting strategy to deal with Eschiti's claims to be the principal chief of the Comanches. The problem was that the Indian Office had issued Eschiti a commission that at least identified him as "a principal chief," which could be interpreted as placing him on the same level as Quanah. The agent in the summer of 1899 who was trying to resolve this delicate matter of protocol was Walker's successor, James F. Randlett, a retired lieutenant colonel. He had had prior experience as Ute agent, and his success in that position undoubtedly explains his assignment to Anadarko, regarded at this time as one of the most unruly agencies in the Indian service. A man of stern mien and unimpeachable integrity, he came to the agency determined to restore order. Randlett quickly sized up the situation, recognizing that if he must have a principal supporter among the Comanches, it had to be Quanah rather than Eschiti. Quanah was, as the new agent informed Commissioner Jones, "much the stronger character." Jones, who apparently had had enough of the constant bickering on the reservation, accepted Randlett's recommendation and issued Quanah a new commission. The first sentence of it read, "This is to certify that Quanah Parker is recognized as the chief of the Comanches."

Despite the best efforts over a period of several years of attorney Shelley, Special Agent Pray, and jealous rivals among the three tribes, Quanah retained his position as not only the dominant Comanche chief but the most influential leader among all three tribes on the reservation. Even with the turmoil of the nineties, Quanah would have occasion to look back upon them as the best years the Comanches had known on the reservation. He himself had emerged as the only Comanche leader capable of meeting the white men on their own economic ground. And as a politician, he had demonstrated skill in dealing not only with his Indian rivals but with sundry agents, inspectors, and commissioners. But what he could not do was slow the congressional juggernaut that was about to break up the reservation.

CHAPTER 8

Trying to Stave Off Disaster

LOOMING over the reservation after 1892, like the proverbial black cloud, was the unratified Jerome Agreement. As the years slipped by and Congress took no action, some of the reservation rank and file allowed themselves to believe that the danger had passed. Quanah knew better and seldom missed an opportunity to lobby against ratification. Over the years his argumentation shifted ground, but he continued to oppose the deal the commissioners had forced on the tribesmen by threatening to invoke the Dawes Severalty Act.

Quanah's initial strategy was to try to delay implementation of the Jerome Agreement as long as possible by slowing the ratification process. Given the steadily growing white population of Oklahoma Territory—between 1890 and 1900 it increased from 60,000 to 400,000—and the demands that population was making for additional land, it is remarkable that ratification was postponed as long as it was. Members of communities surrounding the reservation staged mass meetings at which the cattlemen who were trying to hold on to their pastures were roundly denounced. The Oklahoma protesters were joined by Texans who felt that failure to eliminate the three-million-acre reservation was inhibiting business opportunities for merchants in towns like Wichita Falls.

Speeches of the boomers were sprinkled with references to "boodlers and schemers," "cattle syndicates," and "rich cattlemen." The spokesmen for the land-hungry whites and aspiring merchants and bankers described the reservation in terms normally reserved for catastrophes. "A wall of fire between Texas and her future development," one called it, and another referred to the undeveloped land as "clogging the wheels of commerce." An editor in Kansas City felt impelled to describe the delay in opening the reservation as "a crime against southwestern civilization." Closer to home, a Marlow mass meeting invoked a populist note, resolving that "there is a large and

fertile body of land . . . capable . . . of supporting a dense population
. . . that is being withheld from the masses." It was now argued that
the Indians would profit from the change. A meeting at Chickasha
produced a series of resolutions, including one that stated that the
opening would benefit the Native American by providing "the example of the white settler . . . to stimulate him in his effort at self-
support." This was one of the standard arguments employed to justify
forcing Indians to make room for white neighbors.

To resist the boomers and sooners, Quanah's strategy called first
for hiring an attorney to help slow the ratification process. Accompanied by Lone Wolf and Apiatan, he had gone to Washington for that
purpose in February 1893. This had resulted in the hiring of William
Shelley, who, since he was first approached while still an employee
of the Indian Office, preferred to think of his principal mission as
defense of the Indians from depredation claims rather than opposing
government policy. The attorney, however, did do some lobbying
against ratification and accompanied Indian delegations to hearings
of congressional committees considering the Jerome Agreement. He
would later claim credit for helping block one of the ratification bills.

Every two years the opening of a new session of Congress would
see a bill introduced to ratify the agreement. Usually these did not
get out of committee. It is difficult to apportion credit, although
the Indians, the Texas cattlemen operating through one of their
congressmen, and even Indian service personnel contributed to
blocking the legislation. Agent after agent reported to the Indian
Office that the members of the three tribes uniformly opposed ratification and that a 160-acre farm was insufficient to support a family
in all but a few areas of the reservation. Commissioners of Indian
affairs and secretaries of the interior passed on these evaluations—
sometimes without comment, sometimes with their qualified en-
dorsements—to congressional committees with ratification bills before them.

The Indians protested the agreement at every opportunity. Agent
Frank Baldwin said that the subject came up at every council he
called. Some of the convocations produced memorials to Congress.
A typical one prepared in October 1893 was seven pages long and
contained 323 signatures, the last one Quanah's. The document explained the Indian approval of the Jerome Agreement as having
been obtained by "misrepresentation, threats, and fraud." Chiefs and
headmen were portrayed as having been "beguiled" into signing by
promises to try to get the tribes more money than they had originally
been offered. Some of these memorials attempted to blame the interpreters, particularly the Kiowa Joshua Given, for having misled the
tribesmen. Given died four months after the negotiation of the agree-

ment, according to the Indians because of a curse a medicine man placed upon him by firing an arrow into a representation of Joshua sketched on a deerskin.

Quanah also came in for a share of the criticism. The *Eufaula Indian Journal* carried a story about one of the Indian memorials. The author of the piece attributed the opposition to Quanah, whom he declared was "at the bottom of the new move and a very able body of cattlemen appears to be at his disposal." The reporter went on to say that the charges that the Jerome Commission had used "fraud and force" to obtain the Indian consent to the agreement were too "ingenious" to enable "the lobby to keep the land from settlers and for steers." Another Oklahoma newspaper, the *El Reno Globe*, accused Quanah of a cynical betrayal of his fellow tribesmen:

> Quanah gave as his reason for opposing the opening of the Comanche reservation, that his people were not far enough advanced on the white man's road to cope with the white people. It is strange that he did not think of this when he signed the [Jerome Agreement] and took an active role in securing the signatures of other members of the tribe. There is no doubt that Quanah could successfully cope with the white man in any business transaction, but perhaps he is more successful in dealing with his own people.

Quanah probably did not see these attacks. Even if he had, it is not likely that they would have disturbed him any more than the condemnation from fellow Comanches that he was "really a white man and is getting rich." Big Looking Glass and White Wolf had had a hand in that one.

But Quanah, Big Looking Glass, and White Wolf could join other Comanches in agreeing that opening the reservation to white settlement would be disastrous. And their agent, Frank Baldwin, put it forcefully: "It is their desire that this reservation be kept exclusively for Indians, and this is but natural. They have learned to dread the white man, his avarice and cupidity. . . . They realize that they must learn to . . . take care of themselves . . . but they have an aversion to being crowded on every side by men who have no friendship for the Indian. There is, in fact, no reason why this reservation may not be held intact for Indians."

Quanah was willing to entertain the idea of selling part of the reservation to other Indians, if that was the only way to keep it out of the hands of whites. In the summer of 1897 he was the principal advocate of selling a block of about thirty-three thousand acres to two hundred Wyandots for whom the government was attempting to find a place. As always, he was concerned about price and had a

Quanah and his council, ca. 1900. (*Courtesy Western History Collections, University of Oklahoma Library.*)

good grasp of the bargaining process. An interpreter reported Quanah's dictum in these matters: "He says if a person want to sell anything of his own he got to ask more [than] what it is worth." That deal never materialized, although it was supported also by Big Looking Glass, Apiatan, Apache John, and other leaders of the three tribes.

At the council at which the Wyandot proposition was discussed, Quanah broached the possibility of a law to restrict the reservation to Indians. He admitted that Congress might not go along, as the Jerome Agreement would either have to be redrafted or the Indians permitted to purchase back the surplus land. A proposition with a better chance of success was to expand the part of the reservation controlled by Fort Sill to provide a secure location for Geronimo and his fellow Apaches who had moved there from Alabama in 1894. This was the government's proposal; nevertheless, the three tribes accepted it. Better to share with Geronimo and his people than with the predatory whites.

In the final two years before Congress finally ratified the Jerome Agreement, Quanah in a variety of forums pressed for more land for the Indians. At one three-day council held on the reservation, he joined those calling for the division of the entire reservation among the Indians, leaving no surplus lands for the white settlers. A year later he was arguing for increasing the size of the allotments from 160 to 640 acres. That would still leave some land, and Quanah proposed that the surplus be set aside for children born after the first division. Later that same year another council was being held, this time relating to a contract to be signed with a company to mine gypsum. Quanah, running true to form, wanted to discuss the tribal royalty per ton, proposing that the price be raised from five cents to six cents. He also participated in the customary attacks on the Jerome Agreement, reiterating his argument that the Indians needed more than 160 acres: "I have told all the Secretaries and Commissioners that if anything was done to open up our country for settlement, the Government should see to it that more land per capita be given to us because our country is not a good farming country and we would have to get our supplies from raising cattle."

A joint report from Special Agent Pray and Agent Randlett in December 1899 echoed Quanah's stand. The agents' report went up the line from the Indian commissioner to the secretary of the interior, and from the secretary to the Senate. Pray and Randlett stated categorically that the Indians were not ready for competition with the whites and that to be self-supporting they needed one thousand acres per family. The report had no discernible effect on the members of Congress, although it may have influenced the final shape of the agreement that became law on June 6, 1900.

Behind the scenes, however, lobbyists for the Rock Island Railroad, which had lines on and near the reservation and a major stake in having the area open to white settlement, had been contending with the representative of the Indian Rights Association. This was the premier organization of eastern friends of the Indian, and it had been working, in vain, to increase the amount of land each tribal member would receive. The association's founder and head, Herbert Welsh, in calling the attention of editors to the inequities of the Jerome Agreement, cited the need to begin dealing fairly with the Indians before the United States took on additional dependent peoples in the Philippines, Puerto Rico, and Cuba.

The association did find enough allies in Congress to improve the final version of the Jerome Agreement. It now provided that the Indians were guaranteed at least $500,000 of the $2 million purchase price, regardless of what success the Choctaws and Chickasaws might have in pursuing their claims to the Leased District. (In December 1900 the Supreme Court solved that problem for the Comanches, Kiowas, and Kiowa-Apaches by ruling against the Choctaws and Chickasaws in a parallel case involving the Leased District.) The

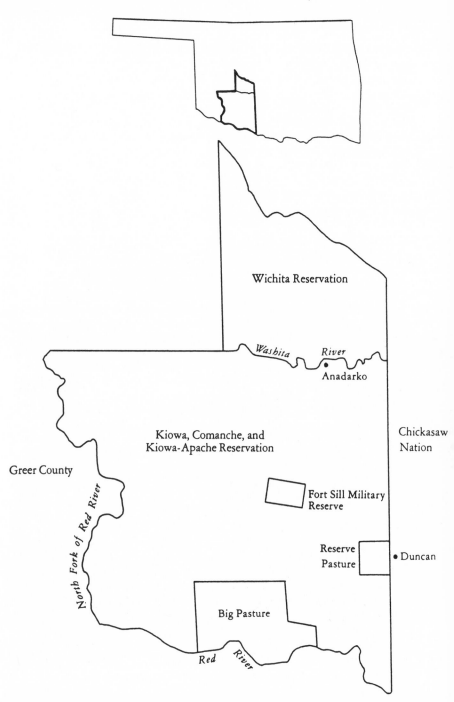

Wichita Reservation

Washita River
• Anadarko

Kiowa, Comanche, and
Kiowa-Apache Reservation

Greer County

North Fork of Red River

Chickasaw
Nation

Fort Sill Military
Reserve

Reserve
Pasture

• Duncan

Big Pasture

Red River

The reservation after ratification of the Jerome Agreement in 1904. (*From Hagan,* United States–Comanche Relations: The Reservation Years, *p. 41.*)

revised agreement also ruled out any depredations claims being made against the $2 million and set aside an additional 480,000 acres of land for the Indians presumably to hold in common. This was over and above the 160-acre allotment each Indian would receive. These were minor improvements in an otherwise disastrous piece of legislation, but the most that could be wrung from a Congress infinitely more responsive to owners of railroads and to land-hungry settlers than to Indians and their very few white supporters.

Quanah learned of the ratification from Agent Randlett, who summoned him, Eschiti, Apiatan, Apache John, and two other Indians. The agent referred to the longtime Indian dissatisfaction with "a bad bargain" but chose to emphasize the amendment providing for the additional 480,000 acres for the Indians. Quanah's resigned response was that it was now law and irreversible. He advised the Indians to select as good land as possible for their allotments and try to make the best of a bad situation. As for the additional 480,000 acres, the Comanche leader observed that it amounted to at least 160 acres per reservation inhabitant and recommended that the Indians be

Quanah and guests at his dinner table, ca. 1900. (*Courtesy Fort Sill Museum.*)

permitted to divide it among themselves. As usual, his contributions to the discussion were the most practical of any Indian present. His fellow Comanche, Eschiti, confined himself to stating: "All these Indians all know that . . . Quanah Parker . . . and myself . . . agreed with Commissioner Jerome and made the treaty and that [Apiatan] did not have anything to do with it."

Lone Wolf and Big Tree, both Kiowa chiefs, were not present at the council. A month before Congress ratified the agreement, they had sought and been denied permission to go to Washington to lobby against the bill. Randlett had reported this episode to Quanah while expressing his own hope that Congress would adjourn without taking action. Even after Congress ratified the commissioners' work, Lone Wolf fought to have the agreement set aside. In this quixotic endeavor Long Wolf was allied with former congressman and former federal judge William M. Springer. Inspired, some said, by the hope of a $5,000 fee, Springer filed suit against Secretary of the Interior Ethan Allan Hitchcock. *Lone Wolf v. Hitchcock* had as its objective a court ruling blocking the opening of the reservation. Three tribunals, however, decided against Lone Wolf, the last one the Supreme Court in 1903. It was a crushing blow for not only the three tribes of the Anadarko agency. The Court held that Congress had plenary power over tribes, regardless of treaties.

Quanah refused to involve himself in the fight that Lone Wolf led, and he was Agent Randlett's principal supporter in his campaign to get the Indians to concentrate on developing their farms. Within a few years of arriving at Fort Sill in 1875, he had assumed the role of ally of the agents, while reserving the right to pursue certain key elements of traditional tribal culture. Quanah had parlayed that combination of seemingly contradictory activities into leadership of the Comanches and relative affluence. In Quanah's final years he would retain much of his political influence, although the basis of his prosperity would erode quickly.

CHAPTER 9

Adapting to the New Order

THIRTEEN months elapsed before the ratification of the Jerome Agreement and the opening of the reservation. For Quanah and his fellow Indians it was a shattering experience. Three thousand white people invaded the reservation less than thirty days after Congress acted, and a year later on the eve of the opening there were fifty thousand sooners ignoring Indian property lines to scout out the best homesteads. Soldiers from Fort Sill cleared intruders from the Wichita Mountains, but they quickly returned in force. Aggravating the situation were the bootleggers and thieves who took advantage of the breakdown of law and order to invade the reservation to steal livestock and dispense to the Indians what Agent Randlett termed "bottled consolation."

Agency personnel encouraged the Indians to select their own allotments. If they failed to do so, the allotting agents would choose for them, presumably from the best land available. Like Quanah, many Comanches in the late 1890s had built houses on land they now requested as allotments. Quanah had made his choice of a homesite primarily because of the age-old Comanche concerns for wood, water, and pasture. The soil of his allotment was far from the best for farming on the reservation, being "gravelly some stony," with less than half of the 160 acres fit for cultivation, according to an appraiser. Not that Quanah ever engaged in farming himself; he was too busy as the chief of the Comanches, a leader in the peyote cult, and a parade or show Indian.

The towns springing up around and on the reservation did not consider their Fourth of July celebrations complete without a contingent of Indians painted, befeathered, and clad in buckskin. As the best-known and most-admired chief in the area, Quanah was sought to recruit other Indians and to lead the parades. At the Lawton Fourth of July celebration in 1902, for example, Quanah was in the

vanguard of the riders, although he had to share the spotlight with
To-nar-cy, who rode beside him, "plump, brilliant, gaudy, and
proud" according to one spectator. Cache, the town only three miles
from Quanah's place, tried to capitalize on his fame by encouraging
him to stage events. On at least two occasions he hosted powwows
that attracted thousands of visitors, both red and white, to a site near
his home. Cache entrepreneurs arranged for some of the Indians to
come there to perform. The highlight in 1903 was a charge by three
hundred warriors on a Frisco passenger train just arriving with people
who had purchased tickets at special excursion rates. Painted, bran-
dishing their bows and arrows, and shrieking their war cries, the
Indians produced near-panic on the train, and passengers screamed
and fainted in the coaches.

Five years later Cache community leaders were again plugging a

Quanah and To-nar-cy, 1901. (*Courtesy Archives & Manuscripts Division of the
Oklahoma Historical Society, 6471.*)

"great Quanah Parker celebration." The association putting on the affair listed Quanah as its president and Knox Beal, a young white man whom Quanah had befriended, as treasurer. The advance publicity promised a wide range of activities, including speeches by noted Oklahomans, bronco busting and steer roping, horse races, Indian dances, and stagecoach robberies. A reporter for the *Cache Clarion and Indiahoma News* spoke of the orators who were "handling all sorts of subjects in a masterly manner . . . a feast of reason and a flow of soul." Among these speakers was Quanah himself, whose message was "filled with wisdom" and "saw a future bright with possibilities for the red man when the government lets him have enough of his money to equip himself with implements and stock so he may farm like a white man." Quanah never missed an opportunity to get his views before the public.

One of those seeking Quanah's presence at affairs was his old cattleman friend Burk Burnett, who reciprocated the favor by arranging permission for Quanah and friends to hunt deer on ranches in Texas. In 1907 Burnett cautioned the chief not to make his hunting trip until the new legal deer season in Texas, as otherwise Quanah would risk trouble with the local whites. That sufficiently alarmed the Comanche that when hunting season arrived he dispatched a rather rambling letter to the governor of Texas. In it he spoke of his desire to hunt deer in Texas and referred to the land grant Cynthia Ann had never realized. He also acknowledged the Panic of 1907: "This year money is pretty hard everywhere." Expressing the hope that he might someday visit the governor, and promising to send a framed picture of himself, Quanah assured the official that "I am a Texas man myself." He continued to cling to the Texas connection, despite the failure of the white Parkers to exhibit much interest in him.

Quanah, nevertheless, was a featured guest at some events in Texas. In the fall of 1908 Burk Burnett had contacted the Comanche, spelling out in careful detail what he wanted of him for a Fort Worth Fat Stock Show appearance the following March. Quanah was to supply about thirty-five Indians, ten of them women, together with two or three tepees. Burnett was particularly pleased at the Comanche's proposal to bring Geronimo, although the old Apache's death in February dashed that hope. The rancher agreed to supply buckskin or palomino horses for all participants, although he offered the Indians no wages, only expenses and "a bully good time." Burnett did tell Quanah to forget the $75 the chief owed him for a horse.

That fall Quanah spoke at the Texas State Fair in Dallas. A paper in Oklahoma City carried the story, although the reporter could only hazard a guess at the subject of the Comanche's lecture: "It's a two-to-one shot that it was the Peyote bean." He went on to remark, in the same light vein, "Quanah is developing powers of oratory that may soon challenge those of Congressman [Charles D.] Carter and Senator [Robert L.] Owen."

The chief would be at the fair again in 1910, this time to help promote "Quanah Route Day." Originally built to service gypsum mines at Acme, Texas, the Quanah, Acme and Pacific Railroad's line in 1909 ran only the six miles from Quanah to Acme. By the following year another thirty-one miles of track had been laid, carrying it to Paducah—a long way from the Pacific. Quanah's publicity work for the railroad somehow gave birth to the rumor that he had invested $40,000 in its stock. As during this period he was barely meeting his living expenses, it was impossible that the chief would have been putting that kind of money in anything. He appeared at the state fair to shill for the railroad promoter for the same reasons that he lent his presence to Fourth of July celebrations and an oil and gas developer's convention in Oklahoma City. It was an opportunity to pick up a few dollars and to dress up in buckskin and feathers and play the role of Comanche chief that he enjoyed so much. Such junkets also enabled him to escape the increasingly depressing and worrisome life he now led on the former reservation.

Given his celebrity, it is not surprising that Quanah would be drafted in 1908 for a cameo role in *The Bank Robbery*, the first movie filmed in Oklahoma. Cache was the site of the bank, and certainly it had no more celebrated personage than its neighbor to the north, the Comanche chief. His role was not terribly demanding. Quanah was filmed as he rode up to the bank in his stagecoach, dismounted, and engaged some local citizens in conversation. After the robbery actually took place, he joined the posse that set out in hot pursuit. Given his constant need at this time to approach bankers as a supplicant, Quanah may well have fantasized joining the outlaws in cleaning out the vaults.

What was the high point of Quanah's career as a parade Indian was his part in the inauguration of Theodore Roosevelt in 1905. Together with Geronimo, Hollow Horn Bear and American Horse of the Sioux, and Little Plume, a Blackfoot, Quanah in warbonnet and buckskin rode in the inaugural parade. Before leaving Washington the chiefs had an audience with the president. It consisted of their shaking hands with Roosevelt and then "gazing silently at the Great Father, who gave them some wholesome advice." Agents, inspectors, Indian commissioners, and secretaries of the interior had been unable to still Quanah, but in the exuberantly voluble Roosevelt he finally had met his match.

A few weeks later Roosevelt did remember Quanah and sought

him out when he traveled to Oklahoma to hunt coyotes. When his train pulled into Frederick, it was met by a crowd of three thousand. A mounted honor guard escorted the president to the speaker's stand erected on the main street. Quanah was a member of the honor guard. Once on the platform, Roosevelt summoned the chief to join him, and the men shook hands to the accompaniment of loud applause. In his brief remarks the president referred to Quanah as a good citizen, expressing the hope that the local people were treating him fairly: "One thing of which I am proud is that I have tried to give a fair deal to every man. Give the red man the same chance as the white. This country is founded on a doctrine of giving each man a fair show to see what there is in him."

While he was in Frederick, however, Roosevelt also gave an audience to James H. Stephens, who represented the Texas congressional district just across the Red River from the 400,000-acre "Big Pasture," where the hunt was held. Stephens was a spokesman for land-hungry whites who were pushing for the United States to purchase the 480,000 acres that had been retained for the Indians in the revised Jerome Agreement. The president was going to find it difficult to devise a "fair deal" that would satisfy his white constituents while doing justice to the Indian.

In the five days that Roosevelt was in Oklahoma, Quanah introduced him to members of his family and briefed the president on the Indian plight. After leaving Oklahoma for Colorado, Roosevelt took the time to write Commissioner of Indian Affairs Francis E. Leupp regarding his conversations with Quanah. "He seems to be a fine old chief," observed the president and then spoke of some of Quanah's concerns. These included territorial officers trying to collect taxes from the Indians and the chief's hopes that, contrary to Congressman Stephens's designs, the tribesmen might retain title to the 480,000 acres. Quanah must have impressed Roosevelt with the unemployment problem among the Indians, as the president suggested to Commissioner Leupp that "we could put in every lease to the cattlemen that a certain number of young Indians should be hired as cow hands." He concluded his letter, "My sympathies have been much excited and I have been aroused by what I have seen here, and I am concerned at the condition of these Indians and the seeming hopelessness of their future." As always, the difficulty would be reconciling a desire to protect the property rights of a small Indian minority with the perceived needs of white Americans.

The disposition of the additional 480,000 acres set aside for the Indians in the revised Jerome Agreement demonstrates the forces at work to relieve the tribesmen of their landed estate. From the beginning Quanah had insisted that this land be apportioned to the Indians, roughly doubling the original 160-acre allotment. It became clear quickly, however, that the real contest would be between the ranchers attempting to hold on to a remnant of the pastures they had leased for about twenty years and the settlers, backed by local business people who saw three thousand potential homesteads in the 480,000 acres.

Within two months of having heard of the ratification of the agreement, Quanah led a six-man delegation to Washington and obtained an audience with President McKinley. The president had a busy schedule the morning the chiefs called and agreed only to a short meeting. He shook hands with them and then spoke briefly about the Jerome Agreement. Before the Indians could be ushered out, Quanah stepped forward, raised his hand in a peremptory gesture, and began to speak his piece: "White man not treat Indian right. Indian want 360 acres. One sixty acres not enough. White man wise, but Indian . . ." At this point the delegation's escort interrupted Quanah, and the Indians were quickly escorted from the room. The official attitude was that the agreement was now law and the only question was how to administer the 480,000 acres.

Agent James Randlett had worked out a compromise that satisfied no one. He divided the 480,000 acres into four tracts, the largest being the Big Pasture of 400,000 acres, which backed up on the Red River. Three smaller pastures were carved from the other 80,000 acres. The 400,000 acres were expected to be leased by several ranchers, who would now quarrel over division of a range that one of them might have occupied before. The other three pastures presumably were to take care of Indian stock. Quanah and his fellow Comanches had insisted on this, as they had the largest number of cattle. The Kiowas and Kiowa-Apaches had relatively little stock and would have preferred that all the 480,000 acres be leased to swell the per capita distribution of grass money. As it turned out, the principal beneficiaries of the Indian pastures were intermarried whites, the squaw men.

While the cattlemen were cutting each other up over who would lease what in the Big Pasture, residents of the town of Duncan were deploring the location of a 22,500-acre pasture immediately west of them. Spokesmen for the town acknowledged that Agent Randlett had acted in the best interests of the Indians but said the pasture "cuts off all ingress and egress to and from Duncan on the West" and would mean "absolute ruin" for the community's almost three thousand residents. Already boomers of other town sites were circulating maps highlighting Duncan's problem in order to advance their own interests. To strengthen their hand, Duncanites sought to enlist Quanah's support for the proposition that creating a pasture west of the town was not in the best interests of the Indians. The Comanche chief refused to play that game, so the white men then turned to Eschiti, who was amenable.

Agent Randlett was most unhappy at Eschiti's action and denounced him to the Indian commissioner as "dull of intellect," "slovenly," and "as of no account in influencing his people in the way of civilized living and entirely unfitted to be a leader." When Eschiti then allowed his name to be added to the list of plaintiffs in Lone Wolf's ill-fated legal action, the agent was even more irritated. In less than a year Randlett had gotten the revocation of Eschiti's chief's warrant on the grounds that he was "non-progressive . . . an obstruction to everything that is proposed by the Department in the interest of the Indians of the Agency." Eschiti had never been a serious threat to Quanah's primacy, and now his ability to compete with the agent's favorite would be further impaired.

Quanah and Agent Randlett worked closely together. The agent kept the Comanche chief fully apprised of problems on the reservation and did not hesitate to call upon him for support, particularly against the Lone Wolf–Big Tree faction of Kiowas during their campaign in the courts to block the opening of the reservation. In turn, the agent favored Quanah when the opportunity arose and attempted to assist him in matters relating to his son Harold and others of the chief's children. Harold, whose mother was Cho-ny, had returned from Carlisle and was handling his father's correspondence, reading him the mail and helping him frame responses. Harold, however, had contracted tuberculosis, and his condition had deteriorated to the point that he was not expected to live long. Quanah, with Randlett's endorsement, petitioned Captain Pratt to release his daughter Wanada from Carlisle so that she might take over Harold's responsibilities. "Quanah has behaved grandly during the late commotion here and is determined to abide by the laws of the land," Randlett wrote Pratt. Carlisle's head responded that Wanada was "an exceptionally good girl, and has intelligence enough to be very useful to her father," and he arranged for her return to Oklahoma.

As Harold's illness dragged on, Randlett manifested real sympathy for the boy and his father, on one occasion prescribing a remedy to help Harold cope with his hemorrhages. The agent was noticeably concerned when smallpox swept through the Comanche ranks in 1901, writing Quanah: "I am very anxious to hear from you and to learn how your family is getting on. It distresses me much that the small pox is working such harm to your people." That it was genuine solicitude is documented by a letter of the same date that Randlett dispatched to one of his subordinates who was responsible for the Indians in Quanah's neighborhood: "I wish you to go over to Quan-

ah's to find out how he is fixed and if anything can be done for him.
. . . I send a letter by the policeman that I want you to read to
Quanah. After you get this I want you to write me every day so long
as smallpox is in Quanah's family, and tell me how they are and if
anything can be done for them." The two wives then living with
Quanah both contracted smallpox but recovered. A shocking total of
173 Comanches, however, died in the epidemic.

Some people saw Randlett as a crusty, arbitrary old man, but he
did seem to have a genuine affection for Quanah. The agent's desire
to assist the chief's children was apparent in two areas: housing
and employment. As he began to look toward a second retirement,
Randlett assured Quanah that, "I hope to get your children all well
established with homes before I leave here." The government had a
housing program through which it provided the lumber and the
paint, and the Indians paid the carpenter. Under this program, Randlett arranged for the construction of a five-room house to be occupied
jointly by Harold and his brother and sister, Baldwin and Honnie.
The agent also responded favorably to Quanah's effort to find employment at the Fort Sill school for his and Weck-e-ah's daughter
Wanada. She was given a position as assistant matron at an annual
salary of $240.

Quanah himself would go on the government payroll at this time.
Agent Randlett initiated the request and made the case for the chief's
meriting a salary, if only for $240 as an "additional farmer" in the
West Cache farmer's district. Randlett spoke of Quanah's valuable
service over the years and his need for additional income: "He was
formerly able to give his services in the way named, but on account
of his generous charity to his people . . . his ability to keep up in this
way of living has been lessened, and as it is absolutely necessary in
the best interest of the service to call upon him frequently for assistance . . . it appears reasonable that . . . the best interests of the service
will be promoted by making him a paid employee."

The Indian Office agreed, and in February Quanah went on the
United States payroll and now would submit claims for reimbursement like any other government servant. Early in 1908, for example,
the Comanche who once had led war parties that covered hundreds
of miles and terrorized the white man's frontier submitted a claim
for expenses incurred in traveling from Cache to Anadarko to sign
papers relating to lease income. His voucher listed 28 cents for a
round-trip ticket from Cache to Lawton on the electric cars, $1.44
for a round-trip railroad ticket from Lawton to Anadarko, dinner
and supper at 50 cents each, and 25 cents for lodging, for a grand total
of $2.97. Three months later a check was mailed to him from St. Louis.
Like millions of government servants before and since, Quanah must

have grumbled at the torturous pace of the reimbursement process, particularly given his growing financial problems.

As they no longer drew annuities, since that clause in the Treaty of Medicine Lodge had lapsed, and only the truly dependent now received government rations, the Comanches were relying on income from funds held in trust by the government and on lease payments. Almost all the Indians had white tenants, frequently permitting them to occupy the houses the government had helped the Indians build. The tribesmen also received per capita payments of grass money. The agents always consulted Quanah about the timing and amount of these and required his presence when the Comanches received them. As many Kiowas and a few Comanches sometimes refused to accept payments as a form of protest, there were political overtones to these affairs, and the agents consulted closely with Quanah about them. To facilitate this, in 1907 the agent had a telephone installed in the chief's residence.

But even Quanah could not always escape the smothering paternalism of the bureaucracy. The chief inherited Harold's allotment when his son died. According to the so-called Dead Indian Act of 1902, Indians inheriting land could get a clear title to it, allowing them to sell the land if they so desired. Framers of the legislation anticipated that this would be both a way to enable Indians to get some capital to develop their allotments and a means of accelerating the flow of land from Indian to white hands. Quanah promptly sold the acreage he had inherited, at a price of $3,025. As the funds were held in trust for him, the chief had to request them and justify his need. He initially tried for the entire $3,025 because "I owe the traders and other store keepers. . . . I also wish to make some improvements on my homestead and buy some cattle, and the balance I wish to place at interest." Randlett's successor and former clerk, John P. Blackman, endorsed Quanah's request, but to no avail. The chief was still considered a ward of the federal government and not to be trusted with such a large sum. Quanah then tried borrowing money and referring the lender to Blackman for payment. The agent refused to honor such drafts and advised the chief not to borrow money, instead to come to Blackman when he needed funds and the agent would release it in small amounts as required. David Jerome, who had closely observed—too closely for his own comfort—Quanah's financial acumen, probably would have been amused at the restrictions the government imposed on his old adversary.

Land had been the issue between Quanah and Jerome, and the chief fought vainly to save the 480,000 acres for the Indians that had been provided for in the revised agreement. Bills had been quickly introduced into Congress, however, to open the land for settlers.

One argument for such legislation was that the income from the sale would make unnecessary further Indian dependence on the government. Quanah opposed these bills, insisting that at a minimum that the Indian children born since the 1901 opening should be allotted land. Agents Randlett and Blackman both objected to opening the 480,000 acres, Randlett describing it as "a breach of faith on the part of the Government and an act entirely in the interest of whites." Nevertheless, Congress finally passed such a bill in March 1906 and sent it to the president. Roosevelt informed its supporters in Congress that he would veto the bill unless they withdrew it. As a result the bill was recalled and amended in a fashion that made it acceptable to Roosevelt and less unsatisfactory to the Indians. Provision was made for allotting the more than three thousand children born since the 1901 opening, and the minimum price to be paid to the Indians was raised from $1.50 an acre to $5.00, a substantial improvement. Offsetting this somewhat, however, was a subsequent law that Roosevelt signed that gave settlers who had opened farms in the pasture adjoining Duncan preemption rights to the tracts they had cleared and cultivated. This is the area from which the allotments for the children would have been chosen, as the tenants had done much of the work in preparing the land for farming. Once again the government had given white men's interests priority over those of the Indians.

When the children's allotments were made, Quanah set up camp in the Big Pasture to help ensure that the parents made good selections for their offspring. He also staked out a claim for an infant son, only to learn that the law opening the land stated that to receive the allotment the child must be living as of June 5, 1906. The son died before that date.

Quanah's complicated marital status caused financial problems as well. A-er-wuth-takum, his fourth wife, had four children by Quanah and separated from him before allotment. She and the chief quarreled over income their two sons Len and Tom, minors at the time, received. As A-er-wuth-takum was caring for the boys, she resented Quanah's using his influence at the agency to divert half of their income to his own account. The chief's defense was that he had used the money to settle a debt she had run up at one of the traders' stores.

Although A-er-wuth-takum portrayed Quanah as a negligent parent, that was not the way he usually was seen, his role in the establishment of a new school district being a case in point. Early in 1908 Quanah approached the Comanche County superintendent of schools about the possibility of getting another school district established. The area in which he lived, which had a number of Indian and white children, was not included in any district. Two years earlier the chief had enrolled his and To-pay's son Kelsey in the school at Cache. But then some of the parents in that school district objected. "The presence of the red youngster was repugnant to the tastes of some of the patrons and they demanded that he be withdrawn" was the report from neighboring Lawton. Quanah then transferred Kelsey to the Fort Sill school, although not at all happy with the situation: "No like Indian school for my people. Indian boy go to Indian school, stay like Indian; go white school, he like white man. Me want white school so my children get educated like whites, be like whites."

The county superintendent discussed the problem with Quanah, and a deal was struck. The chief provided a site for the school on his own allotment and pledged to get local Indians to bear their share of the tax to support the new facility. There was some discussion of hiring as the teacher for the school, White Parker, Quanah's Carlisle-educated son by Ma-cheet-to-wooky. A reason offered for the failure to follow through on this proposal was that Quanah preferred a white instructor so that the Indian children would learn more rapidly to speak English. As president of the new district school board, the chief was in a position to help make this choice.

In his discussions with the county superintendent, Quanah had been assisted by a son-in-law, Aubra C. Birdsong, one of two white men that the chief's daughters married, the other being Emmet Cox. One of the white men who came on the reservation as an employee of Texas cattlemen, Cox first had married a daughter of Quirts-Quip in 1883, and after her death married Nahmukuh, daughter of Wecke-ah. Cox was an enterprising individual who made full use of his connections first to Quirts Quip and then to Quanah. The son-in-law ran large herds of cattle on the reservation with the aid of Comanche cowboys, employed white men to farm eighty acres, and for a time held a license as an Indian trader. He also was one of seventeen people authorized by the Jerome Agreement to "be entitled to all the benefits of land and money conferred by this agreement, the same as if members by blood of one of the said tribes." Cox took advantage of this to exploit a loophole in the Treaty of Medicine Lodge to secure an allotment of 320 acres, twice that which went to the Indians.

Aubra Birdsong came along too late to share in that bonanza, but he did well as a son-in-law of Quanah. A young man of twenty when he went to work on Quanah's farm in 1904, he soon married Neda, one of the chief's daughters by A-er-wuth-takum. Quanah used his influence to get Birdsong appointed to the agency staff and then helped secure his adoption as a Comanche, which would entitle him to an allotment and a share in any tribal funds. At the same time that Birdsong's adoption was approved by the business committee

representing the three tribes, Quanah prevailed upon it to endorse
the adoption of son White's wife, Laura, daughter of a missionary.
Agent Ernest Stecker, who had succeeded John P. Blackman, opposed both adoptions. He was a former first sergeant of H. L. Scott's
Indian detachment and was as well acquainted with the tribesmen as
any white man was likely to be. Stecker argued that both adoptions
were unwise, as their Indian spouses had land and income; to adopt
these white people would be to risk opening the door to many others.
Should that occur, he told the business committee, "there are only
so many pieces of bread," and adding to tribal enrollments was "to
take away part of the share of some of the old Indians who are poor
and uneducated." Nevertheless, Quanah held his ground, arguing
that the business committee had the authority to recommend the
adoptions and that he wanted to have his white son-in-law and
daughter-in-law admitted to the Comanche rolls. When the vote was
finally taken, the Kiowa and Kiowa-Apache representatives on the
business committee joined Quanah in approving the adoptions, although Eschiti and Man-sook-a-wat, the other two Comanches on
the committee, voted against the motion. The negative votes of
these Comanches probably reflected more political factionalism than
anything else.

In these last years Comanche politics were as intense as ever, and
Quanah usually was solidly aligned with the agents. James Randlett,
John Blackman, and Ernest Stecker were honest men, good adminis-
trators, and anxious to do what—in their eyes and the eyes of the
officials in Washington—was best for the Indians. Many of the tribesmen, however, were unwilling to accept white men's judgments as
to what was good for Indians. There undoubtedly also were at work
other forces such as jealousy of Quanah's status.

Agent Randlett's problems with the Lone Wolf Kiowa faction,
which had the support of a few Comanches like Eschiti, led in 1903
to an official investigation of the agency, conducted by Francis E.
Leupp. Leupp was well qualified for the assignment, as he had served
as the Indian Rights Association's Washington agent and in that
capacity had looked into the affairs of several reservations. He also
was a political confidant of President Theodore Roosevelt, who arranged this particular assignment.

After a thorough investigation Leupp rendered a lengthy report in
which he absolved Randlett of the charges that had been made against
him, and he had some interesting observations on Quanah. Leupp
discussed him relative to two other Comanche leaders, Eschiti and
Permamsu. The latter had first entered tribal politics as one of Quanah's lieutenants but had outgrown that role and was now described
by Leupp as leading the most progressive wing of the tribe. Leupp

found him "clever" and influential but not particularly admirable, regarding him as a "professional agitator."

Leupp located Eschiti, "who still wears the cotton sheet around his loins and clings to other aboriginal survivals," at the other end of the political spectrum, with Quanah occupying the middle ground. Leupp described Cynthia Ann's son as "always conscious that he is Indian, but never forgetful that the white civilization is supreme, and that the Indian's wisest course is to adapt himself to it as fast as he can." And when Leupp attempted to evaluate Apiatan, the Kiowa chief, he referred to him as "Chief beyond doubt," but lacking Quanah's "forceful personality."

Responding to a question about the role of chiefs in traditional Indian practices, Leupp acknowledged that Quanah clung to some of the old Comanche ways. He identified only two: the chief's hairstyle and his multiple wives. Leupp defended Quanah's two pigtails as "just double the number affected by George Washington" and invoked the father of his country again in relation to Quanah's much-married state. "In his domestic life, [Quanah] multiplies the responsibilities of the great American exemplar—supports three wives and families at once," declared Leupp. Although he did not discuss Quanah's leadership in the peyote movement, Leupp did defend use of the herb. He reported finding none of the "mescal wrecks" that critics of peyote had described and emphasized the medicinal qualities of peyote.

Leupp, a journalist based in New York and Washington who had been observing the great and near-great political leaders for years, and who had developed a rather jaundiced view of them, was lavish in his praise of Quanah:

> If ever Nature stamped a man with the seal of headship she did it in his case. Quanah would have been a leader and a governor in any circle where fate might have cast him—it is in his blood. His acceptability to all except an inconsiderable minority of his people is plain to any observer, and even those who are restive under his rule recognize its supremacy. He has his followers under wonderful control, but, on the other hand, he looks out for them like a father. . . .
>
> He wastes no time in brooding over the past glories of his race and their ill use by the white people, but recognizes the situation as it is, and is adapting himself to it.

In three areas—hairstyle, multiple wives, and use of peyote— Quanah clung to the old ways until the day of death. When the commissioner of Indian affairs put out an order that Indians give up their long hair, Agent Randlett discussed the new dispensation with

Quanah, ca. 1906. (*Courtesy Archives & Manuscripts Division of the Oklahoma Historical Society, no. 14609.*)

the chief. Quanah asked if there was any law governing length of hair for the whites and reminded the agent that the Comanches cut their hair only in respect to the dead. Quanah also pointed out for Randlett's benefit that the agent's own Chinese servant wore his hair long; if a Chinese could do it, surely an Indian should be permitted. Agent Randlett did not push the matter further.

During his last years Quanah also got relatively little official harassment about his multiple wives. The chief entered the twentieth century with five. A-er-wuth-takum and Co-by had left the Quanah ménage before allotment. Both women remarried. In the first decade of the century Weck-e-ah, Cho-ny, and Ma-cheet-to-wooky chose to disaffiliate, and they too remarried. In his last years Quanah was comforted only by his seventh and eighth wives, To-nar-cy (who sometimes was listed as the principal wife) and To-pay.

The circumstances surrounding both the marriages and the separations are usually unknown. Co-by testified that Cho-ny's parents gave her to Quanah while still a child, and she did not begin to live with him until later. It also is apparent that most of the wives were widows when the chief married them. For only one of the five separations is there evidence for the cause. Weck-e-ah's daughter Wanada attributes her mother's departure from the Parker residence to Quanah's taking a seventh wife—"too many wives," as Weck-e-ah put it bluntly.

Quanah's attachment to peyote was as persistent as his practice of polygamy, although less visible. The all-night services were not advertised, and even Agent Randlett, after thirty months on the reservation, claimed never to have heard of Quanah's leadership role in the cult. The agent was responding to the Indian commissioner, who had received a complaint from a missionary. The commissioner ordered Randlett to investigate; if he found the facts as reported, he should use his "best efforts to stamp out the troublesome and debasing practice." Randlett, in reply, spoke of limited peyote use among the Kiowas but declared the report that Quanah was a leader in the movement was "without foundation." As the old gentleman was a man of great integrity, this statement tells us something about his powers of observation and the circumspection with which Comanches practiced their faith.

Missionaries, who found stiff competition from what would come to be known as the Native American Church, were behind most of the agitation against peyote. Agency officials either claimed ignorance of its use or played down any possibility of adverse effects. Agent Stecker had been aware of its use in his sixteen years among the Indians, and he testified in 1909 that "I do not recall any instance where there was a fatal or serious effect from its use." He also, at the

request of the Indian commissioner, investigated and confirmed the
case of C. S. Simmons, who had operated a carriage repair and
blacksmith shop at Cache since 1901. Simmons attributed his recovery
from a debilitating illness to the curative powers of peyote. Stecker
also transmitted the agency physician's observation that "in all my
experience I have never seen a case of acute peyote poisoning, nor
have I ever known any of the many confessed habitues of it to develop
symptoms which could be charged to the constant use of the drug."

Nevertheless, efforts to ban peyote were intermittent during Quanah's last decade, and he did what he could to oppose them. In
December 1906 he headed a delegation to the Oklahoma Constitutional Convention to protest a plan to divide Comanche County and
to try to head off a proposal to ban peyote. As a reporter for the
Daily Oklahoman described it:

> With pathetic sentences the aged warrior announced that the Indian
> ways were fast dying out, and that the new ways of the paleface were
> coming in. His people desired to be citizens of the new state, but
> hoped to retain some of their old customs. Among these, the most
> important to his mind, and one that was in danger of being taken
> away, was the right to use the mescal bean as a medicine.
>
> "We will use the medicine of the white doctors, but we desire to
> be allowed to use pey-o-te also," he declared.

Thirteen months later, Quanah's concern was an antipeyote bill
introduced into the Oklahoma legislature that would have prevented
its use without a prescription. He led a delegation to the state capitol,
and the Comanche chief testified before the senate committee on
public health and sanitation, defending the herb with which he
claimed an acquaintance of forty years. He also tried to educate the
senators on the difference between the plant that grew close to the
ground and produced the peyote buttons and the shrub that reached
a height between two and three feet and from whose leaves a liquor,
mescal, was distilled. Quanah helped keep that bill in committee,
although a year later he was faced with another antipeyote crusader.

William E. "Pussyfoot" Johnson was a special officer employed by
the commissioner of Indian affairs to combat liquor and drug addic-
tion among the Indians. Early in 1909 the commissioner had responded to continued complaints about peyote by canvassing agents
and physicians in Oklahoma, Nebraska, Iowa, Wyoming, and Wis-
consin. It was to this inquiry that Agent Stecker and the physician
stationed at Anadarko had responded. Other physicians and agents,
or "superintendents," as they now were termed, had been more

Indian delegation to Oklahoma Constitutional Convention, 1906. *Front row:* Tennyson Berry, Codsy, Apache John, Otto Wells, Quanah, Apiatan, Little Bird, Young Calf. (*Courtesy Fort Sill Museum.*)

alarmed at the spread of peyote use, which had led the commissioner to call upon Special Officer Johnson to address the problem.

Johnson's strategy was to attempt to cut off the Indians' access to the buttons. Apparently most of them were being sent through the mails by merchants at Laredo. Quanah was a customer of one Laredo firm, as is evidenced by a letter from Wormser Bros. in which they apologized for the Comanche's receipt of some spoiled peyotes and promised to replace them. Johnson moved to stop shipment through the mails to force the Indians to have to make the expensive trip to Mexico to acquire their stock. Even then he proposed to limit how many buttons they could bring into the country. Quanah discovered this new restriction when a border agent found Marcus Poco, whom the chiefs had dispatched for a supply of buttons, entering the country with 8,000. Poco, a Carlisle alumnus and agency policeman, was permitted to proceed. After he had distributed 3,000 of his stock,

however, a United States marshal, at the request of Special Agent
Johnson, confiscated all but 500 of the remaining 5,000.

As usual, Quanah refused to accept quietly this effort to interfere
with his religious practices. For help he turned to Oklahoma members
of Congress and to H. L. Scott, now a colonel serving as superintendent of the Military Academy at West Point. Quanah claimed that
Commissioner of Indian Affairs R. G. Valentine, Leupp's handpicked successor, had personally investigated the peyote situation at
the Anadarko agency and had agreed to permit Indians to obtain
buttons for their personal use. The chief wanted Scott to intercede
personally with Commissioner Valentine, whom Quanah would call
on in June during what would be his last visit to Washington.

C. S. Simmons, the Cache resident who had become a convert to
peyote, aided Quanah in his approach to Representative Scott Ferris
and Senator T. P. Gore. Ferris interested himself in the issue sufficiently to cause some concern to Special Officer Johnson. Senator
Gore, on querying the Treasury Department about Johnson's harassment of those attempting to import peyotes, elicited a response that
there was no legal ban on the buttons.

Simmons subsequently prepared a brief manuscript entitled "The
Peyote Road" in which he singled out Quanah for praise as a Road
Man, citing one particularly moving service:

> At about three o'clock in the morning, the "silent hour" and the time
> of the greatest manifestation of power, Quanah, the leader, knelt
> before the altar and prayed earnestly. Then, taking the eagle feathers
> in both hands, he arose to his feet. I saw at once that he was under
> great inspiration. His whole personality seemed to change. His eyes
> glowed with a strange light and his body swayed to and fro, vibrating
> with some powerful emotion. He sang the beautiful song, "Ya-na-ah-
> away" (the eagle's flight to the sun), in a most grand and inspiring
> manner.

Members of Oklahoma's congressional delegation had aided
Quanah on the peyote issue, and Congressman Stephens came to the
chief's assistance when he wanted to remove his mother's remains to
Oklahoma. In 1908 Quanah advertised in Texas newspapers for help
in locating Cynthia Ann's grave. J. R. O'Quinn, a son of his mother's
sister, responded with a promise to Quanah that if he would come
to Texas, "I think I can sight you to the place." He concluded, "Well,
I have written to a cousin I never have seen." At last Quanah had
made meaningful contact with his Texas relatives. Within weeks this
was confirmed by an invitation to the chief from another cousin, G.
W. Allison, to attend a family function at Athens in August. As this

conflicted with the date of the big "Quanah Parker Celebration" Cache was advertising, he was unable to accept the invitation. Quanah did not give up on his plan to rebury Cynthia Ann in Oklahoma. Congressman Ferris solved any financial problem that existed by sponsoring a bill that became law March 3, 1909, and authorized the secretary of the interior to expend $1,000 to move Cynthia Ann's remains. Quanah was still apprehensive about what kind of reception he would receive in Texas, and this led him to approach the governor of the state again. Writing in July 1909, Quanah cited his concern about being charged with killing antelope in Texas and being a friend of someone with legal problems there.

Quanah and family members, ca. 1908. *Back row:* granddaughter Nora Cox, granddaughter Nina Cox, son-in-law Walter Komah, daughter Wanada Komah, Quanah, daughter Bessie, daughter-in-law Laura Clark Parker, son White; *middle row:* son-in-law Emmet E. Cox, daughter Nah-mah-kuh Cox, grandson William Murray Cox, wife To-pay, wife To-nar-cy, daughter Laura Parker Birdsong, son-in-law Aubra C. Birdsong; *front row:* granddaughter Ella Cox, grandson Joseph William Cox, son Kelsey, son Chee, unidentified, granddaughter Anona Birdsong. (*Courtesy Fort Sill Museum.*)

The chief concluded with an appeal to the governor, "Would you protect me if I was to come to Austin and neighborhood to remove my mother's body some time soon?"

A year later Quanah did go to Texas and located Cynthia Ann's grave. He delegated to his son-in-law Aubra Birdsong the task of transporting the meager remains of Cynthia Ann to Post Oak Mission cemetery. On December 4, 1910, Reverend A. C. Deyo, a Baptist missionary, preached the funeral sermon, and Reverend A. J. Becker, the Mennonite missionary at Post Oak, supervised the burial. Quanah delivered brief remarks, first in Comanche and then in English. Cynthia Ann, stated her son, "love Indians so well no want to go back to folks." "All same people anyway," the chief observed.

Quanah included in his presentation his standard advice to his people to "follow after white way, get education, know work, make living." He urged that they "learn white God," as he wanted them to "be ready [for death] like my mother, then we all lie together again." The chief must have realized that he was not long for this earth.

Epilogue

QUANAH'S last months were not happy ones. Several weeks before his death he made a confused request for help of Representative Scott Ferris. The congressman took it as a bid for financial assistance and forwarded it to the Indian commissioner with the comment that the chief "was old and in poor health" and expressed the hope that the commissioner "would look over his appeal pretty carefully."

By the end of January 1911, local papers were reporting Quanah's condition in somber tones. A physician had been called in, and his diagnosis was that Quanah was suffering from rheumatism and that while his heart was as yet unaffected, "the advanced age of the chief makes his case a bad one." Less than a month later at the age of about fifty-nine, Quanah died. He had just returned from a visit to some Cheyennes, to seek a cure at a peyote meeting was one report.

He had arrived back in Cache on February 25 in the company of To-nar-cy. During the train ride he had "sat quietly his head bowed and his limbs trembling." At the station he did muster enough strength to walk from the train to the station's waiting room. A physician was summoned, and he supplied a heart stimulant. Quanah was then placed in the automobile of son-in-law Emmet Cox and rushed home. In the first twenty minutes after arriving he was attended both by the physician and by a medicine man. The latter was by the chief's side at the end, having just employed an eagle bone to clear a passage in Quanah's throat so that To-nar-cy might give him water. "He coughed, gasped, moved his lips feebly, and died," was a newspaper's account datelined Cache. The physician concluded that rheumatism had induced heart failure.

Within hours word had spread through the countryside, and mourners appeared to pay their respects. The following morning hundreds gathered at Quanah's pride: his ranch house with its long verandas topped off by a red roof emblazoned with large white stars.

They arrived on cow ponies and in buggies, in farm wagons and automobiles. Those who wished were permitted to file past the flag-draped casket where Quanah lay in his best buckskin. Shortly after noon the large crowd of well over a thousand made their way to the Post Oak Mission in a line a mile and a half long. To-nar-cy traveled by automobile, and other family members squatted in the bed of a farm wagon. At the mission, whites in their Sunday best mingled with blanketed Indians, some of the women carrying babies in cradle boards. Only a fraction of the mourners could fit into the small white-frame church, and many crowded near the open windows straining to hear the ceremony. Reverend A. J. Becker and his wife led a hymn, "Tell It to Jesus," and Reverend E. C. Deyo offered a prayer. Becker then preached, and an Indian translated for the non-English speakers.

At the graveside the coffin's lid was removed to afford one last opportunity to see the dead chief. Then, to the accompaniment of "Nearer My God to Thee," the casket, covered with colorful blankets, was lowered into the grave beside Cynthia Ann's. As he had directed, Quanah was at last reunited with his mother.

The echoes of the hymn had hardly died away before Quanah's heirs begin bickering over his property. It was a modest estate for one so frequently portrayed as wealthy. The imposing white house sat on an allotment of only second-class land. In addition there were two horses and two mules, a coach, a hack, a buggy, a mowing machine, and a hay rake. Personal possessions that would be distributed among the heirs included a warbonnet that went to To-pay, who had made it, a buffalo hide, an engraved pistol presented to Quanah by grateful Texas cattlemen, a shotgun, and a few silver serving pieces. Cynthia Ann's picture that had hung in Quanah's bedroom was given to the eldest son, White Parker, with the injunction that it be passed to a sibling on his own death. To-nar-cy, as the recognized widow under Oklahoma law, took as her portion range rights to one-third of Quanah's allotment. To-pay, who had two children ages eleven and two, got occupancy of the house and the proceeds from the lease of the thirty-five cultivated acres—as long as she remained single. Quanah's debts totaled about $350, but these were covered by the sale of his mules and hack to his son Baldwin for $275, and daughter Nahmukuh's purchase of his stagecoach for $100.

Also at stake at this time was the question of a political heir. Eschiti was Quanah's most prominent rival at the time of his death, and some Comanche leaders expected the former medicine man to succeed Quanah, although son White Parker also was mentioned. Nevertheless, four months after Quanah's death the secretary of the interior passed the word down to Superintendent Stecker to eliminate the

Quanah, ca. 1910. (*Courtesy Archives & Manuscripts Division of the Oklahoma Historical Society, no. 2847.*)

Early version of the Star House, ca. 1893. Note buggies on the porch. (*Courtesy Museum of the Great Plains.*)

office and deal with the business committee and its members from three tribes. This came as no surprise, as the policy for years had been to move toward the elimination of chiefs. Quanah's relatives had provided some support for this, wishing to preserve for him the honor of being the one and only principal chief of the tribe.

The relatives were understandably shocked and horrified at the desecration of his grave four years later. In May 1915 someone opened the chief's grave and rifled the casket. Investigators concluded that three rings, a gold watch chain, and a diamond brooch that Quanah frequently wore on his tie all were missing. At the time of his death the brooch, which had been given him by Texas cattlemen, was highlighted in an Oklahoma City newspaper as valued at $450. Although officials in Washington denounced the "ghoulish outrage" and directed that every effort be made to apprehend the criminals, the perpetrators escaped punishment. The family could only wash the bones, rebury them in a new casket, and plant flowers at the gravesite.

In the late 1920s a move got underway to obtain an appropriation from Congress for a grave monument for Quanah. Secretary of the Interior Hubert Work endorsed the project, lauding the chief as "an efficient factor in leading his people along the road to civilization," one who "discouraged dissipation and savage extravagance among his people and yet held strictly to his native beliefs and ceremonies."

The unveiling of that monument provided another occasion for cele-
brating Quanah. The speaker of the Oklahoma House of Representatives eulogized him as a "beacon of light to a wandering people."
    But the chief himself was still on the move. In 1957 an expansion
of the Fort Sill firing ranges, to accommodate new missiles, encom-
passed the site of Post Oak Mission. Although Cynthia Ann and her
son and daughter were moved to the Fort Sill military cemetery with
appropriate honors, it appeared that even in death they could find
no rest.
    Quanah had had a remarkable career spanning two worlds. As a
youth he had led the life of a nomadic warrior, following the buffalo
herds and terrorizing Texas and Mexican settlements. Within a few
years of taking up residence on a reservation, Quanah had seen the
great shaggy animals disappear before the guns of the hide hunters.
Nevertheless, he would live to see a small herd returned in 1907 to
the Wichita National Game Preserve near his home. "Tell the President that the buffalo is my old friend, and it would make my heart
glad to see a herd once more roaming around Mount Scott," was the
word the chief sent Theodore Roosevelt on learning of the project.
The horse, which had revolutionized life for the Comanches, also
was giving way. Although Quanah still traveled short distances by
buggy, he had become a seasoned train traveler as well and no stranger
to automobiles. Only a month before his death, airplanes made their
first Oklahoma-based flights. His lifetime had indeed spanned two
radically different worlds.
    The transition had not been an easy one for Quanah. He was an
orphan by the time he entered his teens and labored under the
additional disadvantage of being a mixed-blood. These handicaps he
overcame by excelling as a hunter and fighter, the qualities his people
valued most. There were other Comanches more highly respected
and well established in leadership positions when the tribe was united
on the reservation in 1875. Nevertheless, it was Quanah whom his
fellow tribesmen and white officials would come to recognize, in the
next ten years, as the leading Comanche chief.
    Several factors help explain Quanah's rapid rise to the top. Un-
doubtedly he benefited from the novelty of being the son of a Comanche warrior and a captive white woman. Within days of his arrival at
Fort Sill, everyone at the post had heard the story of the young
Comanche seeking information about his white mother. That helped
bring him to the attention of important people, but then he had to
demonstrate real competence to gain their confidence. That same
mixed-blood heritage was no asset in Quanah's dealings with his
fellow tribesmen. Some of them, however, would take advice that
they try to accommodate themselves to their new situation from

The Star House, ca. 1911. (*Courtesy Archives & Manuscripts Division of the Oklahoma Historical Society, no. 3773.*)

someone who made no secret of his adherence to key elements of their traditional culture. Quanah refused to cut his hair and had multiple wives to the day of his death and was one of the most respected and influential leaders in the peyote movement in Oklahoma. He was the classic middleman, a type appearing among the tribes undergoing the trauma of acculturation under reservation conditions.

As a middleman, Quanah derived some of his influence with the Indians from their recognition that he understood the white men well enough to deal effectively with them. For their part, agency personnel found him invaluable because Indians did look to Quanah for guidance, and the white men knew that he generally could be counted on to support government policy. Among the Kiowas, Apiatan played this role, but no one was in doubt as to which chief carried the greater weight on the reservation.

Quanah's close relationship with the Texas cattlemen also was a factor in his rise. He helped them maintain themselves on the reservation for over fifteen years, during which time they provided a steady and dependable income for the reservation's inhabitants. They also contributed to Quanah personally, enabling him to build the large white house that was his pride, as well as presenting him with gifts, including the diamond brooch and the engraved revolver. His trips to Washington, many of which they subsidized, acquainted Washington officials with Quanah as the chief with whom they must deal in matters relating to the Kiowa, Comanche, and Kiowa-Apache reservation.

Although he had fought to delay their acquisition of Indian land, Quanah became an admired and respected figure to the white population of Oklahoma and northern Texas. To them he was a visible reminder of a period that was receding rapidly into history and that with each passing year was being refined into a brave and exciting frontier saga, cleansed of its greed and violence. Quanah in buckskin and feathers and riding a fine horse in a Fourth of July parade had become a living-history statement for his white neighbors.

As the most celebrated individual, white or Indian, in the area, Quanah's handsome home was a beacon to the curious. Even England's Ambassador James Bryce, author of the classic *The American Commonwealth*, came to call at the "star house." The chief extended hospitality not only to his numerous Indian relatives and fellow band, division, and tribe members but to tribesmen from neighboring reservations, as well as the occasional white. It is little wonder that in his last years Quanah was a familiar figure to bankers, from whom he sought a series of small loans. The chief was desperately trying to

Quanah's monument in Fort Sill Cemetery. *Left:* daughter Laura Birdsong; *right:* granddaughter Mrs. Don Wilkinson; *center:* great-granddaughter Donna Ann Parker. (*Courtesy Western History Collections, University of Oklahoma Library.*)

keep himself afloat as his income diminished, while the demands on him as a tribal chief and celebrity grew.

Despite his problems, Quanah continued to display the dignity and courtesy for which he had become well known. With those with whom he was at ease, he displayed a sense of humor and the ability to tell a good story. A keen judge of character, Quanah could describe an individual colorfully and incisively, as when he likened a young white man whom he knew well to a coyote in being incapable of settling down.

Quanah always seemed to stand out in a crowd. He had a commanding presence and took pride in his appearance, whether in native dress or the black suit, white shirt, and tie that he wore on proper occasions. For the photographer he always assumed the dignified stance of a Comanche chief. Most remarkable of all, however, was the confidence that he displayed in moving in the white man's world. No other Indian leader on the reservation even approximated his grasp of political and economic issues. He had the ability to discern the salient issues through the smokescreen of verbiage thrown up by white negotiators, as well as the will to press them for answers to vital questions.

If a leader is, as the dictionary defines it, "a person who has a commanding authority or influence," Quanah clearly qualified. This was grasped by both his supporters and his opponents, who feared him because of his political stature. Francis Leupp probably said it best: "If ever Nature stamped a man with the seal of headship she did it in his case. Quanah would have been a leader and a governor in any circle where fate might have cast him—it is in his blood."

Although it is difficult to compare Indian leaders because of the great diversity of their tribal backgrounds, something may be gained by placing Quanah alongside three contemporaries whose names were even better known across the United States in the late nineteenth century. The trio had made their reputations opposing American expansion. Geronimo, Quanah's neighbor and sometime fellow pa-rade Indian, had succeeded Cochise as the leader of the Chiricahua Apaches fighting to maintain their freedom. In his last campaign, the army had five thousand men in the field trying to corral Geronimo's tiny band of less than fifty Apache men, women, and children. Chief Joseph of the Nez Perce had achieved national prominence when credited by army officers and the press with leading his people in an epic 1,700-mile fighting retreat, while demonstrating unusual regard for the safety and property of white noncombatants. Red Cloud of the Oglala Sioux also had won fame as a warrior chief in the campaign of 1866–67, in which the Indians forced the United States to abandon forts on the Bozeman Trail.

Their physical proximity after the government's decision to transfer
Geronimo and his fellow prisoners from Alabama to Fort Sill in 1894
was one of the few things that the Apache and Quanah had in
common. Quanah came to prominence in the reservation environment, while Geronimo earned a fearsome reputation fighting Americans and Mexicans. Interned and under the direct control of Fort Sill
officers, Geronimo had little opportunity to demonstrate the political
skills that Quanah honed in dealing with rival Indian leaders, officials
of the Indian service, and white ranchers.

Nor did Geronimo generally exhibit traits that earned him the
respect that white men accorded Quanah. Hugh L. Scott, who supervised the Apaches for their first few years at Fort Sill and who
definitely was not anti-Indian, denounced Geronimo as "an unlovely
character, a crossgrained, mean, selfish old curmudgeon." The chief
had bad habits never attributed to Quanah: he drank too much, raced
horses, and gambled. He also had a reputation for lying, not only to
the whites, which might have been excusable, but to fellow Apaches
as well. Geronimo, however, supported the government's schools
and late in life was baptized a Christian. This, however, did not
markedly affect his life-style; he died from the aftereffects of a fall
from his horse while intoxicated.

Geronimo and Quanah shared a pronounced streak of acquisitive-
ness, the Apache being noted for his ability to capitalize on his
notoriety by selling his autograph, items of his clothing, pictures of
himself, and bows and arrows of his own making. Those who wished
the Apache to appear as a tourist attraction, as he did at expositions
at St. Louis, Buffalo, and Omaha, found him a tough bargainer.
Unlike Quanah, who died a poor man, Geronimo was reputed to
have left $10,000 in his bank account.

Chief Joseph, like Geronimo, gained fame as a warrior, although
more humane than the Apache, who was often portrayed as a blood-
thirsty wretch. According to Indian testimony, Joseph's war record
was unduly inflated by the whites. His responsibility when they
clashed with troops trying to block their retreat was to ensure the
safety of the women and children, an important duty but not one
calculated to improve his warrior image.

Although becoming a reservation Indian about the same time as
Quanah, Joseph manifested little of the Comanche's willingness to
adapt. He clung to the old ways to the extent it was possible, refusing
to take an allotment of land, even though that would have enabled
him to move back to the old homeland of the Nez Perce. Joseph also
refused to convert to Christianity, opposed the opening of a school,
and continued to live in a tepee. A somber dignified figure in defeat,

he was an eloquent spokesman for a lost cause. He had surrendered his rifle to Colonel Nelson Miles with the line that still echoes over the years: "From where the sun now stands I will fight no more forever." Colonel Miles, who also had accepted the last surrender of Geronimo, regarded the Apache as an unmitigated liar. In contrast, Miles described Joseph as "a man of more sagacity and intelligence than any Indian I have ever met." But unlike the more flexible Quanah, who became an admired and respected figure among the white people who overran his homeland, Joseph's noble intransigence doomed him to a life of exile from the land he loved.

Quanah and the Oglala chief Red Cloud came from similar backgrounds, both being Plains Indians, and each was a major player after their people were forced to take up residence on a reservation. Older by some twenty years, Red Cloud was publicized coast to coast for his leadership in the successful Sioux effort to close the Bozeman Trail in 1868. When the agent first made Quanah a band chief in 1875, Red Cloud already was the acknowledged leader of the Oglalas, and their agency was for several years designated the Red Cloud Agency. Although the most that his fellow Sioux were willing to accord him was the leading role in the Oglala tribe, one of nine that made up the western, or Plains, Sioux, white officials began to treat him as the chief of the Teton Dakota, who composed seven of the nine Sioux tribes. And Red Cloud, as proud and ambitious as Quanah, was happy to play the part.

Red Cloud faced even greater problems in climbing that greasy pole of political power than did Quanah. An important factor was the sheer numbers of the western Sioux. The Oglalas alone totaled more than the combined Comanches, Kiowas, and Kiowa-Apaches. And just as Quanah faced competition from other Quahadas like Eschiti, and the Yamparikas White Wolf and Tabananaka, Red Cloud had his own rivals. Among the Oglalas they included American Horse and Young Man Afraid of His Horse. Spotted Tail of the Brules had his own agency named after him and was unwilling to take a backseat to any Oglala, and other tribes included chiefs like Sitting Bull of the Hunkpapas, who would have laughed at the white man's claim that Red Cloud was chief of all the Plains Sioux.

While Quanah, despite his many wives, his pigtails, and his peyote, managed to project the image of an Indian leader anxious to lead his followers down the white man's road, Red Cloud more frequently appeared as an obstacle to the government's plans. Quanah, after some delay, became an advocate of the government's education program and in the 1890s preached that the Indians must accept the inevitable, take allotments, and support themselves by farming and

raising stock. In contrast, Red Cloud resolutely opposed education
for his children and grandchildren after at least one of them died after
returning from a boarding school. Nor was he prepared to put his
influence behind the government's program to make his people farmers and stock raisers. He became the darling of the handful of whites
who followed the lead of Dr. T. A. Bland in urging the government
to permit the Indians to set the pace at which they moved down the
white man's road.

Red Cloud, however, was never the diehard reactionary. His pos-
ture at some critical junctures, like the Sioux War of 1876–77, and the
Ghost Dance uprising in 1890–91, could only be termed ambivalent.
Red Cloud declined to leave the reservation in 1876 to join the hostile
Sioux under Crazy Horse, but there is no evidence that he labored
to prevent the steady flow of Oglalas, including his own son Jack, to
Crazy Horse's camp. Likewise during the Ghost Dance troubles, Red
Cloud did not discourage participation by his people, again including
his son Jack. Nevertheless, it was only at gunpoint that the Oglala
chief himself went along, and he escaped at the first opportunity.

By occupying the middle ground in these disputes, Red Cloud
managed to retain sufficient influence with most Oglalas to retain his
position of leadership until after the Ghost Dance difficulties. But by
refusing to come out clearly and forthrightly on the government's
side, he forfeited the essential recognition and support of federal
officials. The Indian power base had eroded to the point that this
was fatal. For the nearly two decades that he survived after the decline
of the Ghost Dance movement, Red Cloud was a cipher in Sioux
politics. As summed up by James C. Olson, the Oglala's biographer,
"Red Cloud's career ended not in violence, as did that of Crazy Horse
and Sitting Bull, it was simply lost in a government file."

While it was easier for Quanah, operating as he was in a much
smaller population with fewer and weaker rivals, he never seems to
have suffered the ambivalence that characterized Red Cloud. On
reporting to Colonel Mackenzie in May 1875, Quanah committed
himself to trying to adjust to the new order, while holding steadfast
to key elements of Comanche social life. That already he had risen
further than most of his peers, despite the handicap of his mixed-
blood, testified to his native abilities and driving ambition. Red
Cloud obviously was a man of talents and ambition also, but he
lacked the mixed-blood factor. Quanah demonstrated from the very
beginning of his reservation life a belief that his white connections
set him apart, made him different. He commented on it often to
white men, and it undoubtedly facilitated his playing the role of
middleman. Francis Leupp was right that "Quanah would have been

a leader and a governor in any circle where fate might have cast him."
Having a white mother, however, certainly altered his behavior in
the reservation environment and the way that white people viewed
him. This had contributed significantly to his successful quest for
power and influence.

Sources

The biographer of Quanah Parker must begin with his mother, Cynthia Ann Parker, about whom much has been written. Margaret Schmidt Hacker's soundly researched *Cynthia Ann Parker* (El Paso: Texas Western Press, 1990) is unlikely to be surpassed.

For Quanah himself, Clyde L. Jackson and Grace Jackson, *Quanah Parker* (New York: Exposition Press, 1963), has been the best available biography. Zoe A. Tilghman, *Quanah, Eagle of the Comanches* (Oklahoma City: Harlow, 1938), contains some details unavailable elsewhere, but Tilghman was not as critical of her sources as she might have been.

For the military operations that led to the Quahadas' taking up residence on the reservation and for their relations with Fort Sill personnel, see Wilbur Sturtevant Nye, *Carbine and Lance: The Story of Old Fort Sill* (Norman: University of Oklahoma Press, 1968). James L. Haley, *The Buffalo War* (Garden City, N.Y.: Doubleday, 1976), is a good general survey of the fighting in 1874–75. For a battle in which Quanah participated, see T. Lindsay Baker and Billy R. Harrison, *Adobe Walls: The History and Archeology of the 1874 Trading Post* (College Station: Texas A&M Press, 1986), and J'Nell Pate, "The Battle of Adobe Walls," *Great Plains Journal* 16 (Fall 1976): 3–44.

Events on the reservation, 1869–73, from a Quaker agent's perspective, are discussed in Laurie Tatum, *Our Red Brothers and the Peace Policy of President Ulysses S. Grant* (Lincoln: University of Nebraska Press, 1970). Another Quaker, Thomas C. Battey, who served as a teacher among the Kiowas, 1869–74, has left his account of those years: *The Life and Adventures of a Quaker among the Indians* (Norman: University of Oklahoma Press, 1968).

E. E. White, *Experiences of a Special Indian Agent* (Norman: University of Oklahoma Press, 1965), deals with conditions on the reservation in the 1890s. Lester Fields Sheffy, *The Francklyn Land & Cattle Company* (Austin: University of Texas Press, 1963), provides information on the leases the ranchers negotiated with the Indians.

I have treated of the Comanche reservation experience in *United States— Comanche Relations* (New Haven: Yale University Press, 1976), and of Quanah specifically in "Quanah Parker," in *American Indian Leaders*, ed. R. David Edmunds (Lincoln: University of Nebraska Press, 1980), and in "Quanah Parker, Indian Judge," in *Probing the American West*, ed. K. Ross Toole et al. (Santa Fe: Museum of New Mexico Press, 1962).

For the Comanche social and political structure I have depended most heavily on Ernest Wallace and E. Adamson Hoebel, *The Comanches* (Norman: University of Oklahoma Press, 1952), and Thomas Whitney Kavanagh, *Political Power and Political Organization: Comanche Politics, 1786–1875* (Ann Arbor: University Microfilms International, 1989).

Omer C. Stewart, *Peyote Religion* (Norman: University of Oklahoma Press, 1987), is the most recent general coverage of the subject. I also found useful Weston La Barre, *The Peyote Cult* (New York: Schocken Books, 1969), and David Wachtel, "Peyotism," in *American Indian Journal* 7 (March 1981): 2–7. Angie Debo, *Geronimo* (Norman: University of Oklahoma Press, 1976); James C. Olson, *Red Cloud and the Sioux Problem* (Lincoln: University of Nebraska Press, 1965); and Alvin M. Josephy, Jr., *The Nez Perce Indians and the Opening of the Northwest* (New Haven: Yale University Press, 1966), were my principal sources for information on Geronimo, Red Cloud, and Chief Joseph.

The primary sources for Quanah's reservation experience are available in great quantity. The most accessible are the Kiowa Agency Files that the Oklahoma Historical Society holds, which it has microfilmed. The National Archives also has microfilmed letters from the Kiowa agent to the commissioner of Indian affairs for the period 1864–80, although only the years 1875–80 contain any material relevant to Quanah. Other sources in the National Archives Record Group 75 include Letter Books of the Office of Indian Affairs, Inspectors' Reports, Special Cases, and Docket 32 of the Indian Claims Commission. Record Group 48 contains valuable Quanah material scattered through such sources as the correspondence of the secretary of the interior's Indian Division. Additional Kiowa Agency Files are available at the Southwest Branch of the National Archives at Fort Worth, which includes, for example, material relating to the disposition of Quanah's estate.

The Fort Sill Museum contains the post commanders' letter books during the period that Quanah became a resident of the reservation, as well as many other items relating to him.

Photographs of Quanah and members of his family are to be found in the collections of the Fort Sill Museum, the Museum of the Great Plains, the National Anthropological Archives of the Smithsonian Institution, the Oklahoma Historical Society, and the Western History Collections of the University of Oklahoma.

The Western History Collections have two other sources of Quanah
material, but they must be used with care: the Duke Indian Oral
History Collection, and the Indian-Pioneer Oral History Collection.
For local newspapers, the best source is the fine collection of the Oklahoma Historical Society.

Index